AUTHORSHIP:
The Dynamic Principles
of Writing Creatively
(c) 1993 Doran William Cannon

by

DORAN WILLIAM CANNON

HANNAH HOUSE, LOS ANGELES, CA.

TITLE:
AUTHORSHIP:
The Dynamic Principles of
Writing Creatively
(c) 1993 Doran William Cannon

AUTHOR:
Doran William Cannon

PUBLISHED BY:
HANNAH HOUSE PUBLISHING COMPANY
SAN: 297-9403
Los Angeles, Ca.
1-800-959-6353

Cover Design: Arthead

Library of Congress Catalogue Number: 93-78294
ISBN: 1-883636-10-8

AUTHORSHIP
Is dedicated to a Great Dad
LESTER A. CANNON
1900-1993

THE AUTHOR
OF
"AUTHORSHIP"

DORAN WILLIAM CANNON

Born and reared in Toledo, Ohio, and educated at Columbia University in New York City, Cannon came to Hollywood in 1971 as a protégé of Francis Coppola.
Since then, Cannon has written over 20 screenplays for producers at most of the major studios. Four have been produced, including Robert Altman's cult classic, BREWSTER McCLOUD. In 1991, three of Cannon's original screenplays were invited into the Archives of the Academy of Motion Picture Arts and Sciences.

In recent years, Cannon has consulted on Screenplay Structure with Major Studios and major producers. He is a Judge for the annual Nicholls Screenwriting Competition. He has mentored at U.S.C. and lectured at U.C.S.B. and consults with screenwriters and writing students on writing projects.

Many of Cannon's unique theories of Authorship have evolved out of his seminars and workshops.

(For information, call 1-800-959-6353)

"The Truth Shall Make You Free."

St. John, New Testament

TABLE OF CONTENTS

ACT THREE- (continued)

AUTHORSHIP:
The Dynamic Principles
of Writing Creatively

PLUS

THE CANNON PLANAGRAM
An Organizational System for Writers
of Screenplays, Novels, or Plays

WRITING:
AN ACT OF DISCOVERY

Writing creatively is an Act of Discovery. When you're doing it right, you will not pre-determine what and how you are going to write. You will allow that Act of Discovery to lead you and guide you, and you will do as your discovery dictates. You will learn what you're thinking and what you are feeling through writing.

Writing is an Act of Discovery, and the discovery will bring your subconscious up to the conscious level and, suddenly, there it is. On paper. And you did it.

What is it to be discovered? Just everything, that's all. Just what you're feeling, what the story is, who the main character is, what his or her inner conflict is, what he needs to do to resolve it, and finally you discover--ho-ho--yourself.

Allow it to happen. That's the trick. This book is about how to allay your fears, how to combine art and craft, how to allow yourself entry into the persona of your own subconscious self, and through that Act of Discovery, how to attain Authorship.

PROLOGUE
CULTIVATING CREATIVITY

Creativity can be cultivated like a fine garden. It requires an understanding of nature, its climate and its seasons, an education in horticulture, a dedication to the tasks, perhaps a "green thumb", and, above all, the passion of a creative artist. Simply enough, if you have this passion, you have the ability, with training and experience, to master the art of writing. If you do not have this passion, all the training in the world and all the perfumes of Arabia will not be able to camouflage your deficiency.

The several aspects of an artistic endeavor relate to one another as do the seasons. Spring would not be so well appreciated without Winter, and Summer is all the more appreciated knowing that its decline will produce Fall. Every art form requires an understanding of not only its art and craft; but there are two other elements even more important, elements which are usually neglected when art and craft are taught. Those two elements are: The Author himself, and the author's Audience and its Self.

The Passion of the author for his garden cannot be pretended; the audience will detect any pretense of passion, and so will the audience applaud the real thing. The reason is that the audience knows passion and is ready, willing and anxious to share the author's passion, together in what I have coined as "... an ecstatic rapport."

It is the artist's task to activate this ecstatic rapport through the vehicle of his own passion, and with the use of the tools of his trade, those primary tools being CATALYST, CATHARSIS, and METAPHOR.

CATALYST is that chemical reaction of the conflicting dramatic elements which thrusts the story into CRISIS and CATHARSIS, which is the difficult process by which the conflicting tensions inherent to the crisis are unwound...and ultimately leading the main character AND the audience towards the remedy which produces a RESOLUTION, which is the final completion of the catharsis. Using Metaphor (via Craft) as the connecting link between the passion of the author and the passion of the audience, "drama" is the final product.

A friend, a mighty contemporary sculptor, told me that he thought Creativity cannot be taught. I disagreed, and while my theories indeed do not teach creativity as such, what they do teach is how Creativity can be cultivated. In that way, the artist can control his or her creativity like a horticulturist tends his garden; allowing his own cultivated creativity to be the primary tool of his art and his craft.

So, then, you will find this textbook to present a far different approach from most of the many books written on the craft of creative, dramatic writing. Most of these books concentrate on the craft and leave the poor student to fend for himself when it comes to getting in touch with his own passion, his own soul, and his own inner conflict. "Inner Conflict" is at the very heart of dramatic literature, and yet it is rarely taught. Unfortunately, it is the other side of the coin which is taught, i.e. "Outer Conflict", aka "Plot", instead of "Story."

In Act Two, Scene Two herein, I make a vital distinction between STORY and PLOT. Simply,

STORY IS EMOTIONAL

PLOT IS PHYSICAL

Once you see the distinctions in their manifold manifestations, you can begin to master the Art and Craft of Creative Writing. Now interpolate the hypothesis to another progression, and remember this--

STORY IS ART. PLOT IS CRAFT.
Or, again,
STORY IS AUTHORSHIP.
PLOT IS WRITING.

Instead of putting "Craft" first, I speak of craft in its place as a tool of creativity. I concentrate on "The Process" ...i.e. the Creative Process, required of true authorship. Understanding the progressive logic of craft, and how to translate your inner feelings into the power of the written word, will allow you to employ craft--effortlessly--as you go along. You need not experience anything approaching "writer's block" as you will learn that writer's block is also part of the process, and as such, can be used as just another tool in your able hands.

You already know craft. You have seen 1,000 movies and read hundreds of novels. Each reveals the writer's craft, but if the noble heart, the righteous soul, the essential spirit and spirituality, the basic logic of the writer did not prevail, craft would be like an empty vase, begging for flowers.

Your best friend will be *Metaphor*, known primarily as a little tool for expressing how one thing is "like" another. In the greater sense, Metaphor is the primary bridge over which you carry your passion. Think of "Body and Soul" as the greatest metaphor ever known...how your Soul cannot be expressed without your living body to contain it. And so, whatever you have to offer to your audience will be the unseen stuff of which drama is made--love and hate, fear and passion...and soul. These must somehow be embodied to be understood. And so, it is your self, dear author, which must be shared in an ecstatic rapport with your audience, and that self must have a body. In the lexicon of your work, "soul" is a metaphor for your Art and "body" a metaphor for your Craft.

To understand and employ your passion through the use of metaphor is what will elevate you from the status of mere "writer" to the status of "author".

AUTHORSHIP- A SCHOLARLY APPROACH

My intention here is to present a scholarly approach to the teaching of authorship, so why do I start out in Chapter One with such witless and ephemeral aspects as ART, INTUITION, PASSION, SPIRITUALITY and ECSTATIC RAPPORT? Surely, when I use the words CATHARSIS, CATALYST, and EPIPHANY, it is then that I am the scholar, but when I use the words "intuition", "passion" and "ecstatic rapport", I am little better than a New Age ectoplast. For what its worth, I see both extremes as being in error, as extremes usually are. A scholarly approach to a practical art is overly intellectual, denying the imagination its due. The greatest scientist of all time, Albert Einstein, said "Imagination is more important than knowledge."

And so it is.

And the opposing extreme, metaphysical dependence on pseudo-science and various belief systems which are so often a substitute for real education, is no better. Nevertheless, there are valuable insights to be drawn from this ephemeral end of the spectrum. Intuition is a tool of all great artists. Spirituality is a place where an artist can connect with the universality of feelings which connect the artist and his audience together. Ecstatic Rapport is the connecting device which links these forces--artist and audience-- together. Since they are totally dependent on each other for spiritual nourishment, artist and audience each require this link.

And so required, at the other extreme, is an intellectual understanding of the tenets of Dramatic Structure. No doubt scholars will attack my words about Aristotle and the Greeks as a direct contradiction, an oxy-moron perhaps, running against the current of the very New Age ephemeralisms I propose. Such is not the case;

in fact, it is the Greek words and their definitions from which I was able to cull and discover my own theories.

Hopefully, my theories represent a practical 20th Century combination of the Greek scholar and, say, the modern painter, impressionist and/or action expressionist, allowing the application of modern technologies to alter the ways and means, and then the rules. Did Greek plays use parallel cutting? You bet. Did Greek epic poems use parallel cutting, you bet. Cutting back and forth between the events in Athens and the events in Troy, creating dramatic tension. Even cutting back and forth between the Gods and the real people in Troy and Athens.

Is the word "Hero" a Greek name? Yes...and "antithesis," and 'thesis' and 'hypothesis' and 'catharsis' and 'catalyst' and 'crisis'? Why did the Greeks not analyze and codify...Passion, Pianissimo, Gusto...the emotional arts.. music, authorship, the feelings of the author. Psyche is a Greek word which, in one inclusive meaning, encompasses Soul, Spirit, and Mind. But where is the Greek word for "heart" and "guts"? 'Metaphor' is a Greek word, but where is the Greek Word for Love and Hate?

Perhaps that is why the Greek Tragedies were so formalized, and why the sense of beauty in their statuary feels so cold and calculated.

Look at the passion of Michelangelo's "Pieta" and the humanity of Michelangelo's statue of David compared to the perfected cold beauty of the Greek statue of Adonis. Adonis leaves us cold, while David is discernibly the son of a mother who loves him. The Pieta is the essence of motherly love. The Greeks examined Truth and Logic, while the Italians (nee Romans) examined human experience. This line of reasoning is not to pit the intelligence of the Greeks against the artfulness of the Italians; only to show the differences. Both, we might recall were great empires, and made many statues in tribute to the greatness of their warriors and their armies.

To put this dialogue to rest, and for the sake of simplicity, let's conclude that the Greeks gave us our "Craft" and the Romans gave us "Art".

Now, let's see what we can make of our understanding of these definitions and distinctions as they apply to the art of writing.

Santa Barbara, Ca. Feb. 1993

STOP!
THINK ABOUT RAISON D'ETRE

Don't write. Don't do it.

Not until you've cleared the idea through the Department of Raison D'être. Raison d'être means "A reason for being."

If you're thinking about writing a romance novel taking place at the North Pole during the time of the French Revolution, and this Eskimo girl has been impregnated by a German explorer who decided to return for the girl against the wishes of his family...in order to escape from the influence of his stepfather, a rug merchant from Lebanon, and start a family at the North Pole because real estate is cheap and prices can only go up, I'd say...don't write it. It doesn't pass the test. It has little, if any, reason for being.

If you're thinking about writing a story about Irving Berlin and how he rose from the gutter to finally write WHITE CHRISTMAS, forget it. It's been done. No raison d'être.

If you're thinking of writing a play about Stalin, how he rose to great heights, how he became ruthless in a ruthless society, and how he finally met his downfall, it might have raison d'être...it's worth examining in different forms...should it be a play? Well, they did one about Stalin, but people are still interested in Stalin. Hm. Maybe. What about a movie? Well, it's doubtful that a big studio would finance it, and it's probably too expensive for an independent. Too bad.

Well, how about a TV movie? Or a mini-series...well, mini-series are usually from best selling books and American topics. And TV movies are usually less serious.

How about Public Television? Hm...could be. But oops, they did a story about Trotsky and Lenin last year and Stalin played a big role in the story.

OK, how about a novel? People are still interested in Russia, Doctor Zhivago was a big hit as both a sweeping romantic novel and as a movie. Publishers like historical novels.

Hm? A novel? OK. If I can get the right slant on Stalin and his wife, maybe this idea can pass the test of ...Raison d'être.

Another consideration, and probably the most important, is to test whether your idea presents a moral value, whether it adds or detracts to the Greater Good. Is it ethical? Do its scenes of violence create more violence in society , or a statement against violence? Does the sexual content reveal the value of love and tenderness in sexual experience or will it promote rape and prurient interest? As an author, you have a responsibility to your audience and to your society to promote personal and social well-being. You have the same responsibility to yourself.

One last word. If your impulse is simply personal and passionate then to Hell with Raison d'être.

Just do it.

ACT ONE

THE AUTHOR WITHIN

ACT ONE: SCENE ONE:
OOPS! IT'S YOU!
THE INTUITIVE APPROACH TO WRITING

As long as you're getting over your fears of being a writer, why not just skip being a mere writer and become an author instead?

An author has learned to allow his own feelings and his own being into the mix. A writer maintains the third person so assiduously as to keep the first person hidden, but for the by-line. An author, however, insists on being there, not so much that his heart is worn on his sleeve, but so that he can count on "transference" (a psychiatric term) to take place. Transference of feeling and soul from author to reader. Call it inspiration if you like. Let YOUR voice and voices speak through your characters and their actions. Don't hold back as if you and your characters are separate. You, the writer, and they, YOUR puppets on a string? Uh-uh, the author must be the puppet on THEIR strings. This will require a self-awareness beyond the norm, but such self-inspection will be well worth it. The truth, as St. John said, will set you free, and in turn it will allow your authorship to emerge.

The author will allow his characters to speak and act through him as a vehicle or as a medium, much like the painter uses his hand and his brush, and when the painting emerges on the canvas, it is his, as author, but it is beyond his own imagination. It must live on its own to be great.

PASSION IS THE KEY

Passion will guide you to your intuition, and intuition will allow you to intelligently sort out, using your mind as your computer, the many mysterious factors you will need to combine into the miracle which you will create.

Not only can you not avoid it, but you *must* bring yourself into the equation. The question is how and why, to know yourself and to sharpen your incursion in a positive way that will enhance rather than detract from the work.

Also,- to make sure you are not using the work as a vehicle for personal therapy. It will always work therapeutically, but you must avoid using it in a self-possessed way. If you are healthy and normal, that will appear, but if you have a dark side, let's say, you may need to focus it to represent *the* dark side, which everyone has in his heart and soul to some degree. You might want to present a main character who is psychotic. Fine, show him, use him, address the issue, but don't make the Work, the Opus, psychotic as well. It will not serve your audience, and it will not serve you either.

ARISTOTLE KNEW

Aristotle was the first to define dramatic principle in his POETICS. The reason he was first was because the Greeks were the inventors of Plays in dramatic form. Previous to Greek Drama were Greek Epics in poetic form. Aristotle's basic work was to differentiate his definition of Truth from Plato's theory that Truth is "Absolute" to his own definition that Truth is "Relative," Plato posited that no outside influence could debase "Truth"; and Aristotle believed that truth can *only* be true in relationship to those outside elements affecting it.

In today's terms, the dialogue between Left Brain (Plato) and Right Brain (Aristotle) presents an ongoing quest for artists of Drama and Comedy. Tragedy has basically evolved into today's Drama. Aristotle distinguishes Tragedy from Comedy because Tragic characters are noble and Comedy's characters are "low."

Aristotle recognized that drama is about "man in action," a profound concept then, and in the modern medium of the movies, even more profound. Man in action must be acted (acted, action, get it?) rather than recited, and by exciting PITY and FEAR, drama (nee Tragedy) will produce relief from those emotions. CATHARSIS is the Greek word that Aristotle defined as representing that RELIEF FROM FEAR AND PITY.

As we shall see in later chapters, CATHARSIS is the single most important concept for the dramatic author to understand. It is the key to the Kingdom of Drama. Usually thought of as that which the audience must experience and derive from seeing a movie or play, it is so much more than that. It is the stuff of the drama itself, and it is the stuff which the author must also experience to write effectively. It is at the core of what I call "The Holy Trinity". (See Act II, Scene III)

For our purposes, we can define the elusive meanings of "Pity and Fear" as Dramatic Conflict, basically, the combined inner conflict of the main character, the protagonist, and it is through Catharsis that his inner conflict is and <u>must be</u> resolved.

By example, Aristotle also writes of how Fear and Pity can be "purged" (i.e. Catharsis), through... Music! What a great reference for the dramatist who may, throughout his work think of himself writing Musically. Music may be the greatest metaphor for Drama. Francis Coppola, whose father, Carmine Coppola, a great classical composer, no doubt absorbed music in his soul as a child, and transposed it to the rhythms of screenwriting and directing. Movies *are* a composition.

Understanding dramatic form as musical form is to understand Plot Construction. Understanding that music, at it's best, is meant to evoke feeling, and again, in modern terms, the right (feeling) side of the brain vis-a-vis the left (thinking) side.

Aristotle also understood the dynamic necessity of PLOT, CHARACTER, and STORY in drama. These, together with Beginning, Middle and End, are the basic building blocks. Beginning, Middle and End are Action. Plot is Action, Character and Story are Reaction. Hmmm? Aristotle called PLOT, the "psyche" of the drama, and by so doing, he unwittingly caused modern dramatic analysts to confuse the true definitions of story and plot, a mix-up which I will have the audacity in later chapters to re-define with a clarity which should help dramatists immeasurably in understanding how to write.

Starting now, it is my understanding that by PLOT, Aristotle really meant, in our terms, STORY. And the difference is like Night and Day, Yin and Yang, Truman and Dewey. Sorry Mister Aristotle, it is STORY which is the "psyche" of drama. Plot is simply the physical body in which the psyche operates. Plot has arms and legs, and STORY moves them along from one place to another.

As an author, you should write those definitions on the blackboard of your mind, one-hundred times, till it sinks in.

Now, when Aristotle speaks of the two essential moving elements of PLOT, we can understand those two esoteric words so much better. PERIPETIA and ANAGNORISIS are elements of Story and have nothing to do with Plot. Peripetia can be quickly understood as a "reversal of fortune" and better understood as that which happens when the main character's course of action, designed to create a certain result, instead, produces another.   And not just another, but in fact, the diametrically opposite result.

THELMA AND LOUISE,   set out to relieve themselves of their stultifying relationships with the men in their lives, but instead of relief, they meet with their worst case scenario: rape, manslaughter, and fugitivity.   In modern drama, even novels, but most particularly in the movies, this is done on action.   In Greek drama, it would be told in terms of "expectation" and betrayal of that expectation, but in modern terms that would be defined as "suspense", and suspense is a form of Action.

PAINTING FROM THE INSIDE OUT

Quoted from an article by a water-color painter Pat Denman in
AMERICAN ARTIST MAGAZINE, Sept. 1992

"My most thrilling experience with water color came
in the third grade, when my classmates and I were given
an assignment to paint a simple Christmas-tree
ornament hanging from an evergreen twig. As I wet the
drawing and touched the paper with a brush charged
with paint, the water picked up the pigment and literally
swirled it around the ball, creating a perfect, glistening
ornament. I was struck with amazement as THE PIC-
TURE ALMOST SEEMED TO HAVE PAINTED ITSELF!"

In her adult life as an artist, Pat Denman explains
that it took her some time before she was able to "ensure
the excitement of discovery", to face her "moment of
truth". Listen up:

"My method is painting from the inside out; in
other words, I paint the response that comes from
within me, rather than the image of the subject that
actually appears without. Visualizing an image in my
imagination and striving to express that idea with paint
creates an exciting partnership between painter and
paint... the paint often seems to have a will of it's own!"

Do you think, author-to-be, that this process is the
special reserve of those who use such visceral tools as
brush and paint and canvas... or, in the case of musical
composers, tools so abstract, notes and bars, and time,
and rhythm, that the tools you have at hand, mere
words, are not just as powerful as the painter's tools or
the composers tool's?   I believe that you know this, but
you may be unsure as to how to use them.

Look at the painting titled LYRICAL LIGHT on page
23. Do you feel the power of it's emotional theme (it's
"story")? Surely its style and theme, and basically skilled
techniques could translate to a particular movie story or
music.   Look at how romantic it is?   Would it
correspond to Mozart or to Beethoven.   More so
Beethoven? Certainly not Wagner. It is romantic and
pretty, and not beastly and dark, and operatic, like
Wagner. It is also very feminine, and seems to glorify

life's best potentials. So, what movie then? ON THE WATERFRONT? Heavens, no! MARY POPPINS? How about SABRINA, with Audrey Hepburn? Getting closer? How about.....?????

Notice how the painting juxtaposes the light and dark images, how they mirror each other, and present the basic conflict full face, and how ultimately they also resolve the conflict, focus in an area of resolution... our eye is drawn center, where the lights and darks converge, and merge molecularly, bringing the dynamic Yin and Yang forces together in resolution, and finally focused on the harmony, which was always present from edge to edge of the canvas, and symbolically, from beginning to middle to end. The artist has used her tools in no less dramatic fashion than you, as author, can do with the tools at your command. In the end, only one thing will count. What feelings you will have evoked from your audience by your opus. There is no other measure.

The artist, Pat Denman, further explains:

"...as I work, what is most important to me is what FEELS right or wrong... although I ALWAYS KEEP IN MIND THE BASIC PRINCIPLES OF WHAT MAKES A GOOD PAINTING... Working this way doesn't mean I don't spend a good deal of time thinking about and nurturing an idea before starting to paint. Many ideas simmer on the back burners of my mind before coming to fruition in a painting.

"Occasionally, a painting takes a completely different direction than what I had originally conceived. If the image on the paper is exciting enough, I allow it to continue to take the lead and follow my impulses in accord with what is happening."

IT'S THE CREATIVE PROCESS

What this artist is describing is The Creative Process. She uses her instinct, but she always keeps in mind the basic principles of technique. In a nutshell, THAT is the creative process, and when you, as author, use it in writing, and you develop your technique to the point where INSTINCT and TECHNIQUE are fused as one, you will have become a great writer.

Read what she has said above, again, and this time transpose the word "scene" for painting. Think of every scene you write as a painting. Apply the artist's stated techniques.

When writing a scene, "...what is most important to me is what FEELS right...",--"...KEEP IN MIND the BASIC PRINCIPLES of..." ...is what makes a good scene work.

"Working this way doesn't mean I don't spend a good deal of time thinking about and nurturing an idea before starting to..." write. You too, as author, should let a scene ruminate in your mind for a time before you write it. But once you sit down to write it, as you know, I advise you to start in at once, write it instinctively and as quickly as you can, without allowing any so-called Writers Block to take over your mind.

Opposite Page >

"LYRICAL LIGHT"
(1989   20 x 40")
Watercolor by
Pat Denman

ON CHARACTER -
OOPS! IT'S "YOU".

"You" are the character you know best. "You" embody all the elements of Character. There is a part of you which is loving, a part which is hateful, a part which cares, and, depending on your background and your psychological makeup, you will react in certain ways to certain stimuli.

The characters you create, are just like "You." Each has the capacity to love, hate, feel pain and fear; and each will react to stimuli according to his personal disposition. Even though he might react differently from yourself, there is an element in your own disposition which will suggest to you how that character will react. You can depend on it, and you can use it in your work.

The problem for most writers is how to break through the many layers of deceit and distruth in their own selves to get to the honest truth about themselves, so that self-truth becomes a valid tool to create "character" in the protagonist and the other population of his drama; even those characters, perhaps especially-those characters who are most unlike you, whose oppositeness and uniqueness can be understood by you by the transpositioning you are able to do based on your own understanding of.,.....guess who? Yourself.

This involves an act of self-exploration and discovery. When successful, this exploration of self will result in your writing on a much deeper and more intense level. The solutions to your own problems often offer the solutions to the problems of your own characters, and vice-versa. Since creative writing itself is an Act of Discovery, once you have found the key to writing this way, you will easily begin to "discover" yourself and your characters almost simultaneously. That's when you are "cooking."

The danger is in writing for self-therapy. Writing is such a powerful tool for self-therapy that you must be careful to create characters who are NOT yourself. Your characters must have an observable universality which keeps the balance between being of their own mind and yours.

A Los Angeles psychotherapist specializing in helping creative writers, Rachel Ballon, Ph.D.., states in an article in the Writers Guild Journal of June 1990:

"In my practice I have seen parallels between the rich characters in scripts created by talented writers and the characters my patients describe in their life scripts. I now believe powerful characterization needs to come from within, and that it's imperative that writers let themselves be vulnerable, receptive and open to taking risks in their writing."

To continue that line of thought, one could really say that the writer takes the greater risks when he or she doesn't "..take risks." The risk of writer's block, the risk of weak characters resulting in a weak story and an unsold manuscript is by far the greater risk. Ultimately, the risk of an unfinished masterpiece, or even harder to take, the risk of an unstarted masterpiece is the greatest risk of all. The fear of that act of self-discovery is the one greatest stumbling block for neophyte and professional writers alike.

Later on, I explain the essential difference between STORY and PLOT. Story is emotional and Plot is physical. Most of my new students start by telling their story in terms of Plot, and they fail sadly in the process. When they begin again, telling the story in Emotional Terms only, and add a few plot elements as they go, the story starts to come alive. It's so simple. Story precedes plot, and the self-discovery of Character precedes Story. So, where do you begin? You begin with "YOU."

Dr. Ballon asserts--" Each person has a private self where all thinking, feeling and imagination reside, and a public self which carries our observable behavior. These different selves can be in conflict with each other, and writers have to be both aware of their rich inner world, and accessible to the deep passionate characters who live there."

So, be careful...don't let the missing link to your success be "You."

ACT TWO

DRAMATIC STRUCTURE

ACT TWO
SCENE ONE:

BEGINNING
EXPOSITION
SET-UP
CATALYST

MIDDLE
CRISIS
CATHARSIS
EPIPHANY

END
REMEDY
CLIMAX
RESOLUTION
(EPILOGUE)

SCENE ONE:
BEGINNING, MIDDLE, END

There are many parallels for beginning, middle and end. In dramatic form, the one common denominator is that beginning, middle and end flow through TIME. For our purposes, pages of text are the vehicle to describe TIME. Our primary reference for beginning, middle and end is the THREE ACT FORMAT.

Parallel to the Three Acts are:

ACT ONE   ACT TWO   ACT THREE
(SET-UP)   (CRISIS)   (EPIPHANY)
CATALYST- CATHARSIS - RESOLUTION

CATALYST, CATHARSIS, RESOLUTION   are the three ACTIVE (Action) elements of your drama.

Understood and used well by yourself, as author, they are powerful forces to carry an emotional theme from beginning to end. They are the bridge from the only organic, living, human source of this drama, which is YOU, AUTHOR, to the only other organic, human element involved, which is YOUR AUDIENCE. It is the life, the love, the meaning that you breathe in to this inert object that creates the magic of drama. Think of the Sistine Chapel, where God reaches out to Man, touching fingertips, and Man takes on life. God is the author of man, just as you will be the author of your screenplay or novel.

Another parallel configuration is:

PAST   PRESENT   FUTURE

When you set your drama in the PRESENT, it is actually the MIDDLE oF ACT TWO of your character's complete dramatic history. Even so, his Present history breaks into three acts, a beginning, middle and an end. This illustrates that every portion of a drama has a beginning, middle and an end; and so those components and their emotional line, i.e. Catalyst, catharsis, and resolution, become the basis of every sequence and within that sequence, every scene, and within that scene, every separate piece of dialogue. In a scene, we can call this structure- THRUST, BATTLE, PAYOFF. It becomes a piece in the puzzle. It is always used EMOTIONALLY to push the story forward.

Briefly, the following definitions are useful to us, as authors:

CATALYST-

Once you have set-up the circumstances in that foresection called EXPOSITION (see below), you will move forthwith into CATALYST. In chemistry, the catalyst is an inert agent which causes a chemical change or acceleration without the agent itself undergoing any change. In human interaction, it is an action between two or more persons or forces producing a change in circumstances. In drama, ideally, that change of circumstances will be the driving force of the drama. The more dramatic force it has, the more drama will be produced. It must be an honest catalyst derived from the honest and credible revelations of the Exposition. If it is not honest, it will produce MELODRAMA, an undesirable over-amplification of drama.

Practically, if it comes in the form of dialogue or some other non-graphic and relatively inactive or passive form it will produce less thrust and less drama than if it comes in the form of something visual and impacting such as a gun being used to shoot someone, as in THELMA AND LOUISE.

CATHARSIS-

Another Greek word, well understood by Aristotle, catharsis is defined as a cleansing. Interestingly, it is first defined in drama as an effect which relieves or purges the emotions of an audience. So, your job as an author is to produce an emotional catharsis in your audience, and how do you accomplish this? By purging the emotions of that main character, the PROTAGONIST, of the conflicts and jeopardy he has experienced after the CATALYST. In psychiatry, (which arrived as a revolutionary technique dealing with he human emotions just about the same time as Naturalism on the stage {i.e. Ibsen} and a revolutionary art form, the movies, came into being), it is defined as "the discharge of pent-up emotion so as to result in the alleviation of symptoms or the permanent relief of the condition." Catharsis is the emotional turmoil, or conflict, which must exist, and which leads to EPIPHANY (see below) and RESOLUTION.

Catharsis IS Drama. It is the compelling factor of the whole of your work. Even though I have consigned it to that area the Second Act where the main character digests the force fed Crisis, it also serves as the overall dramatic thrust of the entire work- what it means, how it will likely come out, in a sense, the prime of its life. In that sense, even though the Second Act has the feel to the author and often the audience that it is only in the way of the resolution, it is the very path to the resolution, and just as important as Act One or Act Two.

RESOLUTION-

Interestingly, in medicine a Resolvent is a REMEDY which causes the resolutions of a swelling or inflammation. In music, resolution is the transition of the harmony from a dissonance to a consonance. Metaphorically, these definitions provide us with the best clues to the resolution, or last act in drama. There has to be a remedy, a strong dramatic event which provides the transition from catharsis and Epiphany, resolution and the final harmony.

Augmenting the above three major stages :

EXPOSITION-

Exposition "exposes" the circumstances. In and of itself, it is dead weight. It may reveal dramatic and emotional content, but it does not MOVE the story. It reveals character, circumstances, set and setting, back story (i.e. past history), the dreams and aspirations of the main character, and the EMOTIONAL CONFLICT inherent in the story to come. The story itself has not yet been set into motion. Elements of the story may be foreshadowed, cloaked in a bubble of mystery. Flaws in the Protagonist may be revealed, even the Fatal Flaw. No 'time and now' revelation should be wasted or be lacking in meaning. We don't want the audience to be confused with a red herring, unless the red herring is useful to the story. E.M. Forster had a character, Mrs. Moore, in "PASSAGE TO INDIA" remark, "Oh, I love a mystery, but not a muddle." Foresster laid out his method as an author through the mouth of his character... that he will always provide the audience with a good mystery, and the audience can count on him to know that what may seem confusing for the present time, will be cleared up in the course of the mystery.

EPIPHANY-

Classically defined as that moment when the Protagonist reaches an enlightenment. It is a turning point, and a point of no return. It is that point by which the main character resolves his internal conflict and soon finds the REMEDY by which he can resolve his external conflict, and for the author, it is the means by which he can satisfy the audiences need for cathartic resolution. For example, Willie Loman decides that there is only one way out of his dilemma. He has tried and failed at every other way, and he now clearly sees that committing suicide, so that the insurance money can help his wife and kids, is the way for him to go. Oddly, the same resolution is chosen in THELMA AND LOUISE. But, there are differences. What are the differences? And What can we learn from the differences?

ACT TWO
SCENE TWO

YINS
AND
YANGS

ACT TWO: SCENE TWO
THE TWO SIDES TO DRAMATIC STRUCTURE

If you think carefully about this, you will be able to use this fundamental in every aspect of your authorship.

The two sides are the SEEN and the UNSEEN. This can also be called TEXT and SUBTEXT. One side cannot exist without the other. Metaphorically, let's call the two sides BODY and SOUL. Just as your protagonist has a body, he has a soul, and that's the part we, as authors', are really interested in portraying. And in dialogue, when we write TEXT, we want always to keep in mind, the SUBTEXT. And when developing the CONFLICT in our story and in our character, we must remember that the OVERT CONFLICT will represent the COVERT CONFLICT, and when we create our CHARACTERS, we must portray their stated aspirations and intent, but remember that they also have a hidden agenda, e.g., If I can become rich (overt agenda), Susan will marry me and people will respect me (hidden agenda).

Okay, so the next question becomes how can you, as author, portray what is unseen, what is not heard, what is felt but not shown? And the answer is simple, true, and if kept in mind, it will be your most valuable ally. The answer is that you portray that which is not seen by what is seen, what is not heard by what is heard, what is not felt by what is seen and heard. It is in an ecstatic rapport with your audience that you can do this. You and your audience, by your common and universal experience in real life know what the other is, or has felt at some time, in the most essential ways, fear, pity, lust, love, anger, etc., and each, you and your audience knows what represents those feelings, those hidden secrets, and those hidden agendas when the audience sees those actions on stage or screen. When an actor prepares for his role (see AN ACTOR PREPARES/Stanislavski) he finds those actions which will represent to the audience emotions already experienced. This is what you must do as an author. A primary example is the fundamental comparison between STORY and PLOT.

STORY V. PLOT

STORY
IS
EMOTIONAL

• • • • • • •

PLOT
IS
PHYSICAL

STORY AND PLOT

What is the difference between STORY and PLOT?

STORY is EMOTIONAL.
PLOT is PHYSICAL.

You cannot see the emotions, so you use plot as the vehicle to carry the story along.

For every unseen element, there is a physical element at your disposal which will represent it and carry it, whether it is Character, story, dialogue or otherwise. Plot is one of the tools of your trade. Like the brush and paint and canvas of an artist, these tools, these techniques will spell out an emotional response in the viewer.

And it is the constant vibrational resonance between Story and Plot which creates dramatic tension.

It is Yin and Yang.

THE YINS AND YANGS
OF DRAMATIC STRUCTURE

*STORY AND PLOT; ACTION AND REACTIONS;
ACTIVE AND PASSIVE; GOOD V. EVIL: LIGHT V.
DARK; BODY AND SOUL, FEMININE AND
MASCULINE; RIGHT V. LEFT; INTUITION V.
KNOWLEDGE OF FACTS; MELODY V. HARMONY*

The list goes on; while the point remains the same.
Like Alternating Current, the Yin and Yang of your
authorship are what will produce a dynamic, thrusting,
suspenseful, and emotional dramatic structure.   The
YIN is in the abstract, and its counterpart, the YANG, is
the physical manifestation of the YIN. Story needs Plot
to reveal it, Good needs Evil to define Good, Masculine
needs Feminine, Action has no value without Reaction,
and Light needs Dark.   Your job is to reveal what cannot
be seen, through what can be seen and heard.   Think
metaphorically, write metaphorically.   Think of your
screenplay as Body and Soul. You know there is a soul,
but it cannot be revealed to its holder without a body,
and then one's soul cannot be revealed to other people
(an audience or the other characters in a drama) without
a body. Your story is the soul of your screenplay, and the
Plot is the body.
When you devise your Story, think of it only in
emotional terms. That Jack and Jill went up the hill is
Plot. Should they hold hands while they go up the hill
reveals, through action, that they love each other.
That's Story. Now, when they get up the hill, and Jack
falls down and breaks his crown, the plot "thickens" and
the story becomes more emotional. We feel sorry for
Jack. We liked the guy. And now, to complicate
matters, Jill comes tumbling after. We knew they loved
each other. We like them both. They failed to meet
their goal, which was to fetch a pail of water. The whole
town was waiting to get that water, because, due to the
pollution (cause of the Outer Conflict) produced by the

corporate interests at Big Corp., children in the hospital may die (the Stakes).

Now the story is becoming strong. Because of the conflict, the emotional stakes have gone up. How those emotional stakes will be played out can only be carried forward with plot. And, in turn The Plot requires to be played out on Action. And then, to be valid, each Action requires a Reaction, either by the characters in the drama, the audience, or both. When it is by both, it is higher drama than just one or the other.

As an author, you might choose carefully as to which moments will have the reaction of both... for dramatic emphasis. Jack gets up (his action) sees Jill is hurt (her reaction.) Goes to her... She sees that he's coming (reaction)... He pulls her up, together they fetch the water and start down the hill. We know they will be heroes to the town people, but somehow, the payoff does not seem strong enough.

Why? There is still something gnawing away at us, and at Jack. We, the audience do not feel that the Internal Conflict within Jack's character has been resolved; and neither does Jack. If he does not resolve it, his relationship with Jill will never be quite right. Externally, he has solved his love issue, and he has gotten the water to save the children, but his inner conflict, the demons within his own soul have not been conquered. Well... that's an inner conflict, a question of character. Its inert, its passive. Screw Jack, let him live his life out in pain! Uh-uh. The author says NO!

So you, as author, have a responsibility to your character and to your audience. You know the principles of structure, and you have a tool available. You have created Jack's antagonist, Green Giant, and so in one last great battle, the author presents Jack with the Green Giant as he returns with the water. If the Green Giant defeats Jack, we have Tragedy; unless Jill picks up his sword and kills the Green Giant—we have a bittersweet drama. But, if Jack defeats the Green Giant, we have a fully resolved drama.

THE HOLY TRINITY

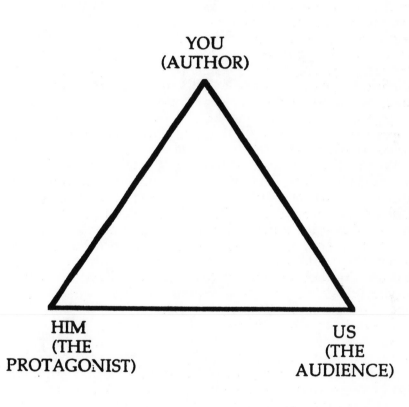

YOU
(AUTHOR)

HIM
(THE
PROTAGONIST)

US
(THE
AUDIENCE)

THE HOLY TRINITY

You are the author of your dreams. And, you are the author of your words. And, you are the author of your works. You are responsible for the meaning the reader derives, and if the reader is confused, you are responsible for that. The clarity and meaning of your works will reflect the clarity and the meaning of your self. On a more spiritual level, the clarity and meaning of your works will reflect the clarity and the meaning of your SOUL.

You are the author of your dreams. You are the author of your soul, and you will be the author of your destiny. Destiny is your destin-a-tion. And the destination of your protagonist. His destiny is in your hands, and your destiny is in his. But you are the author of your character. He owes his "life" to you, and so the only person responsible for the success of your character and your screenplay is yourself. If your focus is on "success", you will fail. If you focus on the transference of your dreams, your best hopes, your belief in the Holy Trinity, yourself, your character and your audience, success will follow in your wake.

The Holy Trinity is the intertwined fate of YOURSELF, YOUR CHARACTER, AND YOUR AUDIENCE (i.e. THE READER).

This triangle is the basic building unit of your work. Buckminster Fuller used it to create the Geodesic Dome. The Egyptians used it to build the pyramids. If it was good enough for them, it's good enough for you.

The strengths of your technique will depend entirely on the strength and the good health of your design of for using this Holy Trinity. In Yoga it would be the Chakra, wherein the spine is a series of vertebrae, so to speak, each representing a separate aspect of your being, starting with your Sexual Persona at the lowest level of your genitalia and bowels, and proceeding upwards, through your Head and Soul, to your Breath, to your Mind, and beyond to your Universal Spirituality.

Ask yourself the question, "What do I feel? What do I want my audience to feel? Is it the same "feeling" for both? Is that what my main character is feeling, experiencing, trying to deal with?"

Then, ask yourself if you understand the anguish your main character is going through? Will the audience understand it? If the answer is that you're not sure, then you, as author, are not really sure of your main character's inner conflict. To test this, make a reference check... first to yourself, like Stanislavski, try to *feel* what the main character would feel and then write it down in a list of characteristics, how those feelings might translate in terms of physical characteristics and physical behavior, then work backwards. Is this the main character you want, that you believe in, that represents YOU AS AUTHOR? That represent YOU, if you were he/she?

You can work forwards and backwards to arrive at conclusions. Consider Handwriting Analysis, evidently a true science, not a whacko new-age cult. Handwriting Analysis provides well defined clues to the personality of the writer. It is now used by corporations to screen job applicants, and by governments to determine the personality flaws of people seeking security clearances. Presumably, if you work hard to change your personality, your handwriting will change. Conversely, if you change your handwriting over time, your personality will change.

In that same fashion, you can discover and rediscover "character." By changing the "characteristics" of your main character, his/her character/behavior will change also. You, as author, are never stuck with your character, allowing him/her to drag you around after him, like a sick marriage. You have the ability to change him/her, but it must start with your own inspection of yourself. What are your own character flaws and characteristics? Are you a "sucker" for a beggar on the street, but thick-skinned when it comes to feeling sorry for your own alcoholic sister? How, then, did you react when your sister was in need of help? Did you turn away from her, but then, after someone reminded you how kind your sister was to you in a childhood incident, you cried your eyes out (catharsis) and then moved to help your sister (remedy and resolution)? And, if not yourself, then do you know a person such a thing happened to? Are you able, like an actor, to get under that person's skin in order to perform as an author?

Do you know such a person? Does that suit your character, or has that kind of characteristic shown up in your main character without your really having planned it that way? Do you want to go with it, or eliminate it? What are you trying to say as an author? Does this characteristic suit what you are trying to say, or does it tend to undermine it? On the other hand, does it complicate the story in an interesting way that you may be able to use... to create dramatic irony, or to create sympathy where there was too little to get your point across?

Remember, the audience will not judge your authorship intellectually. It will judge it emotionally - if the audience laughs at a comedy, if it cries at a tragedy, if it *feels* satisfied when it leaves.

It is the Holy Trinity -- you, the audience and your main character must feel (through Catharsis) satisfied at how the drama unfolded and how it resolved.

ACT TWO:
SCENE THREE

BETWEEN
THE
ACTS

SCENE THREE:
BETWEEN THE ACTS

There once was a cigar called BETWEEN THE ACTS, a little cigar, just enough puffs for the sophisticated smoker to puff on between the acts. After all, Hemingway told his biographer, Lillian Ross, that it was not what was in the lines, but between the lines. What was not seen, the real stuff, the subtext. Like brain matter, it's not the sweetbreads that have value. It's the "thought" in those human sweetbread that count. So, while you're puffing your cigar between the acts, you have the opportunity to reflect on the act you just saw and the act which is to come. I knew there was a point to this.

THIRD ACT FIRST

Why do I explain the Third Act first?

Because the Third Act must be known and understood in order write the First Act, and the Second Act cannot be known and understood until the Third Act and the First Act are understood. The Third Act is your payoff. If the First Act and the Second Act do not predict the Third Act, they are invalid.

And the Third Act, typically, is the act that fails. What a shame to write two great Acts and then see all you good work go down the drain. Or write a two act drama, end it at the end of the Second Act, and fool yourself and your audience with a false resolution. I saw this happen in THE COCKTAIL PARTY, by A. C. Gurney, in which a burning question brought up in the First Act, i.e., whether the protagonist, the son, the playwright, was actually the son of his father or the son of his mother's lover. At the end of the Second Act, the son mentions that he realizes he is really the son of his father, because he now knows that his father really loves him. Problem is, Mr. Gurney, you as author answered the question intellectually, but not emotionally. You didn't allow the emotionality of the central question to play itself out, revealing, consciously to me as a dramatic structurist, and subconsciously to the audience, that you have not resolved your own emotional family dilemma.

You have resolved it no doubt intellectually, as did your protagonist, but you have not resolved it emotionally. You needed a Third Act for that. Instead, you wrote a socially acceptable two-act play, applauded by stuffy audiences still in denial all over the suburban landscape of America. The reason these audiences accept your two-act, unresolved play is because it represents a family dysfunction, much like the families of so many of the people in your audience. But, had you given them the pleasure of the Third Act, the act which resolves the protagonist's, and therefore the playwright's, and therefore the audience's inner conflict, you would have done those in the audience, emotionally available to accept the message, a great service...the ability to experience emotional catharsis and resolution. Something to take home and deal with in their own lives. But, sir, you cut us off at the emotional pass, and kept your characters, yourself, and your audience in the dark ages. Too bad.

The Third Act IS Action. While you, the author, have told the story "on action" from the beginning, it is the Third Act when the protagonist takes over from the author, and takes Action in his own right. Or, as John Lennon suggested in "His Own Write," he is like a child who has now grown up, no longer really needs his parent, except for occasional guidance, and he must cut loose and take care of his own problems on his own. And, you as parent, can do little but watch and pray that your offspring has learned lessons well. And, if you have been a caring parent through Act One and Two, you will have reared a healthy child.

Finally, this is the act of REMEDY and RESOLUTION, where, through the rising tension of his CRISIS which has produced his CATHARSIS and his EPIPHANY, he realizes that the remedy he must employ will be to fight and defeat the antagonist, in whatever form the antagonist might have been represented. If it is a mythological dragon, he will have to fight it and defeat it in order to "save" both the damsel in distress and, heroically, less importantly, himself. But of course saving the damsel is the PHYSICAL MANIFESTATION which actually represents the saving of himself. It's Yin and Yang. To save himself emotionally, something which cannot really be seen and felt physically, he must save something greater than himself in a physical way. It is okay if he saves himself first, by defeating the dragon, but his greater purpose will be to save something or someone greater than himself. You may be wondering--okay, it works that way in grand and heroic mythological stories, what about the little stories, slice of life type stories. It's the same, text and subtext.

So think out the major elements of your Third Act before you get stuck with unusable "activity" in the First Act.

THE FIRST ACT SECOND

Once you have discovered the Inevitable Ending to your Third Act, you can discover the elements of the First Act.

There are three basic phases to The First Act:

First, the CATALYST. The catalyst is at the end of the First Act, and the events of the First Act must thrust forward to the Inevitable Ending of the First Act, the catalyst. A catalyst is the explosive thrust resulting from the chemical reaction of the basic conflict, mixed with a specific plot event, resulting in a catalytic reaction. This catalytic reaction provides the thrust to launch the main character into a crisis at both the Story level and the Plot level, simultaneously. This crisis begins the Second Act. In a movie script, the catalyst will come between pages 25 and 30, no later. Like a symphonic composer, you will time your First Movement to climax (with the Catalyst) at about this point in the script.

This is good news, because it forces you to think through the basic scene structure of the First Act.

Once the catalytic event is chosen, and often the catalytic event you choose will represent the social or psychological problem you want to essay philosophically (see THELMA AND LOUISE.)>, you may go ahead with structuring the First Act from page one.

WRITE ON ACTION

Don't begin with boring information. You will have plenty of time and space to blend in mere information and back story with action.

Separate in your mind the difference between the action and mere information, then make sure that each scene has action at its base. In THELMA AND LOUISE it's easy. They want to get out of town, and they go, and they go farther, and the farther they get out of the safety of the home nest, the more we feel a sense of jeopardy for them. That's what action produces. A reaction...in this case, the reaction is a sense of jeopardy. The audience feels it more than they do, and so the audience is rooting for them to be careful.

BEGIN IN THE MIDDLE OF SOMETHING.

Give the audience the opportunity to guess what your story is about, let them piece the puzzle together as it goes along. Keep them guessing.

REVEAL YOUR MAIN CHARACTER'S INNER CONFLICT

Even if the main character is not yet introduced, you may introduce an inkling of his inner conflict. Perhaps you reveal it in some symbolic plot conflict. This is more important than showing the circumstances, the house, the street, the town etc. This means that your primary concern to begin is STORY, those emotional issues and sparks that the audience wants to know. Everything else is mere plot. THELMA AND LOUISE begins with a prosaic phone conversation immediately revealing their individual inner conflicts, Louise dying spiritually in the diner, and Thelma confined like a young tigress in the cage of her home. She is the tigress and Darryl, her husband, is her keeper. Together, the two women spark with the excitement of running away, getting out of town. Bang! The characters are exposed and the conflict is announced by the author.

Now that the audience is prepared for a good roller coaster ride, you can thread new elements and characters through one scene after the other. Each of these scenes must further complicate both the inner (Story) conflict and the outer (Plot) conflict to thrust your main characters towards the final event of Act One, where the chemical reaction will take place.

K.I.S.S.- KEEP IT SIMPLE, STUPID

Remember the difference between drama and melodrama. Don't overstate your story in order to set-up and maintain "action." Action can be subtle. An animal in a cage is in action, because we know that the animal's every little move is motivated by its desire to escape. If your main character's inner conflict is well defined in story terms, you will not have to worry about creating "action". It will always be there at your command.

Okay. Act Two.

THE SECOND ACT THIRD

The Second Act acts as a bridge, draining the tension of the First Act and the Third Act into its receptacle and slowly re-pouring the dramatic tension into the Third Act. Since the Third Act is shorter, the tension nearly runs over the rim, and we can barely drink it fast enough to keep it from running over.

The Second Act is an act of crisis and catharsis and epiphany. Crisis is the conflict suddenly redefined by the catalyst. So, now the story is charged, catalytic, electrified in CRISIS. The action now rides on the crisis and the story becomes magnified and magnetic in reaction. Yin and Yang, the energy flows like alternating current at about 220 volts. And so, the tension builds. Unlike the Third Act, where the "chase" is told in parallel cutting within the same fast-paced tension building sequence; the tension is built in alternating scenes and sequences, building tension, but in the Second Act, the tension is the tension of CRISIS AND CATHARSIS, not Resolution, and so it is more action than reaction, more plot than story, more nervous energy than explosion.

REALIZATION;
BUT NOT YET RESOLUTION

The action moves inexorably toward an inevitable ending, the ending of the Second Act, where the final catharsis has carried us to the epiphany in which the main character realizes who and what and how. He gets the answers to the questions, catapulted by the catalyst into crisis, it is a conclusion at the end of Act TWO, because he now **realizes** himself, but he has not **resolved** himself or his story. As it has been from the beginning, he has no choice... he must resolve through action. He must physicalize his intellectual and spiritual Epiphany in choosing a physical remedy. For author, character, and audience, it must be active and on action. As author, you have no choice. Can it be a mere conceptual remedy? Uh-uh. Not in the novel, the play or the screenplay. On the screen, the action is more obvious, but it is action nevertheless in the novel, when the inevitable takes place. Or on the stage, when the drama heightens and the dramatist must use every device at his command.

It is a physical plot device, like a prop. If he gets into a car, it will be as a vehicle to his inevitable ending. If he runs, the sidewalk will be as a treadmill, inevitable as it was for Dustin Hoffman struggling to complete Ben's determined destiny with Elaine in THE GRADUATE.

The Second Act is the receptacle for the mystery which ravels into a tight ball at the end of the First Act, and which loosens during the second act, we can see the strands wrapped over each other now, and we're un-tangling the knots... then suddenly, in the Third Act, it unravels, at first too fast to be safe, our hero could trip over the strands, and then finally the string is all laid out... and it is safe for the author to quit, the main character to go on with his/her life in a transformed state, and the audience to go home satisfied that there is always a solution, a re-solution, as it were, to the mysteries of life.

So, re-solution is then finding the solution again, and again, and the drama will always present a solution, and thus a re-solution. Solution is absolute, the story is absolute.

THE THIRD ACT AGAIN

In your Third Act, the main character must find his remedy to the crisis he experienced in the Second Act relating to the dilemma and conflict he first discovered in the First Act. Once he utilizes the remedy, he will be swept along inexorably to a resolution he cannot predict. We, the audience, have sensed the inevitably of this resolution from the beginning, indeed, we rooted for the protagonist to find the very resolution that we knew all along would be his salvation. We were never able to articulate it, but we felt it in our hearts. So it is best, as author, to know what the resolution will be. Mind you, you do not yet need to know how it is manifested physically, because it is a story value; resolution is emotional, not physical. Ultimately, you will need a physical vehicle on which the resolution can ride to it's inexorable conclusion, but you don't need the plot device (the physical) to start with. You choose the physical vehicle in the First Act. They must match. Sometimes you will actually "bookend" your drama with the same physical irony at the beginning as at the end. For example, your protagonist starts his story at the age of nine on the porch of his parents' house in Peoria, and at the end, he returns to that porch at the age of seventy-six. What has happened in between is his story.

THE INEVITABLE ENDING V. THE PREDICTABLE ENDING

Your ending must be inevitable, but if it is also too predictable, you've failed. How can you produce an inevitable ending, i.e. boy who met girl in first scene, fell in love with her by end of First Act, worked hard to get her in early Second Act, but loses her at end of Second Act, then must regain her in the Third Act. We KNOW that he's going to regain her in the Third Act. We just know it because it's right and it would be wrong if he didn't. It's inevitable. But, that need not mean, that it must be predicable as well as inevitable. What, you say, how can that be?

The answer lies in the Yin and Yang. Story vs. Plot. Seen and Unseen. Emotional vs. Physical. And in this instance, what is inevitable can be thought of as emotional. We will be so **happy** when he regains the girl. It is STORY. But what is predicable can then be thought of as PLOT... **how** he regains the girl. How he regains the girl need not be predictable, in fact, you need to invent a plot device that is unpredictable. How so? You must surprise the audience with this plot device.

And so, we will call it THE TWIST.

THE TWIST

The audience remembers that the girl's Aunt Sadie lives in Pittsburgh, and the audience knows that Hero is going to Pittsburgh on a business trip, so he will see the aunt there and she will try to patch things up with her niece. Probably on the phone, since the niece has run off to Denmark with a prince. God only knows where she can be found. So, he is in Pittsburgh and he calls on the Aunt. They sit in her sitting room having tea. He tells the Aunt how much he loves her niece... that it was all a big mix-up. Do you think that you could find her, and if you find her, could you talk to her when you go to Denmark next month? If she hasn't already married the Danish prince she ran off with, that is? The Aunt nods knowingly at his every statement, tells him that she sympathizes with him, but she is powerless. In matters of love, the heart is one's only guide. Sadly, he is just about to leave when The Girl, his girl appears from another room, saying she heard everything and she now knows where her heart is. They embrace, and blah, blah... the ending is happy. Just as HAPPY as we knew it would be all along, but we have been surprised by the twist --the girl was in the other room and not in Denmark.

CLIMAX

Sex relieves tension, and also the climax in fiction.

The climax is THE MOMENT OF RESOLUTION. In technical terms, you've been building tension through parallel cutting between the action of the protagonist and that of his antagonist, and finally, as the action gets faster and tougher, cutting between the two elements, yin and yanging like sexual partners, the climax arrives. Thank God.

This is the business of the Third Act, but it's more than just a payoff, as the payoff of scenes are called. It is the culmination of everything you have worked for. The culmination of the protagonist, he has won. He has achieved the pinnacle, he has graduated. He has saved the day. He realized what needed to be done in his Epiphany at the end Act Two. Then at the beginning of the Third Act he decided what action he could take to remedy the impossible dilemma he has been in since the catalyst at the end of Act One. He's been working hard, and so, what a relief it is to reach the climax.

He saw the girl, he wooed the girl, he defeated the competition for the girl, allowing him to seduce the girl and now he has won the girl.

Sexual tension is relieved. The audience doesn't just applaud. It cheers. It is what the audience wanted for its beloved hero. And it was you, the author that gave this gift to the audience. Author! Author! they scream, you appear form the wings for your short bow, then go back into your lonely room the next day to write another one.

That you as author have returned to your room satisfied, is like the coda or the tag of the screenplay as well. Somehow the relief of tension at the climax is not the end, it is the climax of the story, but like the moral of the story, an added moment must be added where the characters react to the climax, tell of their satisfaction, and we, the audience approve.

So, the climax is not the end, it is the beginning of the end. We know who won the big game and by what score, and now we must realize the reaction of the characters to the action.

NOW you may return to your room.

ACT TWO
SCENE FOUR

CHARACTER
(SIGH)
AH, CHARACTER!

ACT TWO: SCENE FOUR
CHARACTER IS INERT AND UNSEEN

Character is INERT and INTERNAL. As such it is in the category of STORY, which is EMOTIONAL. How, then can we make it known to the audience, and by the same token, how do we make the character of the Protagonist known to the other characters around him? her?

The answer is to give a body to Character, literally to embody it into a physical person. This is a powerful tool in the author's hands; and so how well he uses it will determine the success of his screenplay or novel. He starts with a clean slate. He can do as he pleases with what he has at his disposal, and what he has to begin is a choice of elements which also require physical body by which to reveal and express his themework. The author now has the opportunity to express his idea, his concept and his theme and any other conceptual elements he may need to express.... by using the physical presence of a dramatic "character."

By so embodying his inert ideas in this inert form, character, he may then physicalize the ideas, and in turn activate the story with the external manifestation of his internal character. Sounds like gibberish, but these theories represent the keys to the author's domain. (To the experienced and intuitive writer, it is gibberish, because he already knows all this!)

Even for your own purposes, you do not need to know the deep psychological factors of your main character's persona. You do need to describe the physical factors, age, education, social strata, the type of places he has experienced, what disappointments and triumphs he may have encountered, etc., whether he has a limp (and why), athletic, near-sighted, wears glasses and more. Verbally, what is his accent, his patois, what does he do with his time during the day, the nights, the weekends, Sundays?

The sum total, in its complexity, of all of this, as it is revealed, will tell the audience and the characters around him as much as they will need to know, until

Over time, you will reveal his OPEN AGENDA (...to become wealthy), and his HIDDEN AGENDA (...to use his newfound wealth to gain power over other men and/or to please his father). Finally, you will reveal his REACTIVE AGENDA, i.e. his POINT OF VIEW. His Point of View, in reaction to events of the plot, will create his story, and will drive the story. And on the basis of his reaction and point of view, he will ultimately take action to defend or repair the damage done to his hidden agenda (as it is presented as his OPEN AGENDA).

It is often stated that dialogue is useful in revealing character, but dialogue is the lowest form of action. In itself, it does not reveal character. It hides character, and clothes or reveals hidden agenda. It is the ACTION and REACTION surrounding dialogue that tells the story. It is the subtext of dialogue, the ideas and emotional themes you as author want to reveal through the deceit that is dialogue. that tells your story and pushes it along.

THE PROTAGONIST - RULES ON CHARACTER

Your protagonist is your main character, and we must be rooting for him to succeed in sorting out his personal inner-crisis and the outer conflict as well. I met with an accomplished writer, a woman who had taught fiction writing for several years at a small Southern California college. She'd had several novels published. She consulted with me because she wanted to try her hand at writing screenplays. And she had an idea for writing a screenplay about Hitler... in which Hitler was the main character and we experienced his rise from the time of an epiphanical moment in his youth, when he had a vision that it was his destiny to lead the world. I pointed out to her that Hitler cannot be the main character, since his character is the antithesis of the protagonist. Since Hitler is a well known historical character, there would be no way by which dramatic license could be applied to adjust his character to become the protagonist. I showed her that the actual protagonist in a story about Hitler would have to be someone else, someone who is close to Hitler and able to observe him.

For example, as we have shown above, the protagonist may be a divided psychic profile, as in THELMA AND LOUISE, where each is a different side of the same persona. Thelma is Feminine and Louise is Masculine, Yin and Yang.

In the case of Hitler, using dramatic license, supposing Hitler had a brother (or a childhood friend... or?) who, in their younger days had shared a dark life view with Adolph, who shared his beliefs in astrology, his quest for world power, and his egomania. As time goes on, however, and with his brother secretly at his side, providing encouragement, Hitler goes on to gain power. But, as time goes on, his bother begins to see how Hitler has become powermad, he does what he can to dissuade him from his course, showing him, perhaps, how much talent he once had as an artist, how much compassion he once had as a person. But, it is for naught, and in the end, Hitler's brother returns to the small town of their youth, and marries the girl they both left behind, the girl who loved them both. Hilter's brother, then, is our protagonist and we see in the resolution of his brother's character what Hitler could have been. He has not been able to reform Hitler and has not been able to change the course of history, but he has resolved his own personal dilemma. We, the audience, rooted for him... knew what he had to do, and when he finally did what we knew he had to do, we feel satisfied emotionally. Both the protagonist and the audience have experienced Catharsis, the final proof of success in drama.

Still, to arrive at this "final proof", your protagonist must pass muster. Here are more Tests for Protagonist:

1. His Inner Conflict must be the most pronounced of any other character. His Inner conflict must not be trivial. It must be the stuff of which drama is made. And the larger it is, then the larger the scope of the author's canvas. It must, in it's profundity, match the canvas. A tiny inner conflict, the kind which provides a "moral to the story", might be suited to a short story or a one-act play, for example. But a major inner conflict, the kind of profound moral and personal dilemma experienced by Gandhi, for example, would require a massive canvas. It cannot be trivialized.

2. The Protagonist's Inner Conflict must be fodder for the process.. Identifiable Inner Conflict, represented physically by an outer conflict for himself, and a separate Outer Conflict, represented in the larger drama at hand, the drama in which all the other characters are involved ; and he must experience a single Catalytic Event, which in turn creates a crisis at three or more levels at once (Inner Crisis, Outer personal crisis, and Outer dramatic crisis, see more on this in THE HOLY TRINITY)... and then, of course, thrust through Catharsis, Epiphany, Remedy and Resolution... on both inner and outer levels.

3. His Inner Conflict must translate to Theme, Structure, Story, Plot, and Raison d'être. As author, you must inspect all these requirements and see if there is enough substance to carry through 107 pages, and almost two hours of screen time. Ask yourself a critical question. Is the audience going to care? And are they going to care enough to maintain it's concentration appropriately? As author, you must inspect your idea and your main character to see if he/she is an authentic protagonist.

THE PROTAGONIST'S ANTAGONIST

Your Main Character is the PROTAGONIST. And your protagonist's main character is his ANTAGONIST. Together, they represent the conflict or the conflicting forces of the drama. In a war story, a great general needs a great general of the opposing forces to help spell out his story. HIS-STORY. In a love story, the object of the main character's affection is the antagonist in a classic battle of the sexes. And so, Yin and Yang, the main character is in a polarity and then, perhaps, a continuity with his antagonist, whereby each is the other side of the coin, so to speak. So, one's antagonist is, in important ways, a mirror image of himself, of his other side. The antagonist does not exist in a vacuum. He is not merely the new Psychotic Killer in town this year, rather, he is the dark side of the detective-protagonist who is trying to nail him.

Martin Scorcese's 1991 version of CAPE FEAR is a recent example of that. As audience, we are not informed of this in literal terms, we are informed of it emotional terms. Robert de Niro's character is a very scary ex-con Antagonist to a basically frightened type of family man as played by John Lithgow. See how the protagonist is basically "frightened" and so his antagonist is "scary." As author, we have the responsibility to understand this Yin and Yang relationship, and to find ways to expose it, use it, tell our story with it, let the story tell itself through this Yin and Yang interplay, and ultimately, reveal the epiphany to the main character whereby he will find a way to defeat his "other side". In CAPE FEAR, the final resolution is told in an extraordinarily physical battle between the de Niro and Lithgow characters. The battle's intensity reflects the intensity of the inner conflicts within each character. In the end, of course, Good wins over Evil...not because it is right, but because the main character had resolved his inner conflict, i.e. his Fatal Flaw, but the Antagonist was unable to overcome his Tragic Flaw. Destiny was at work in dramatic terms.

In a love story, the main character will not find a way to defeat his antagonist, which is the woman he loves, but to defeat, with a remedy of resolution, to defeat the forces that have polarized them, and to bring them together. In that way, he has defeated his antagonist and has found harmony.

You must never underestimate or overestimate the power of your main character, you must know and use his character within the confines you have created for him/her. Your character IS real, becomes real, when he/she lives and behaves within the confines of fictional art. The laws of fictional art dictate that your character, and therefore your story, must be credible and convincing, and you must not allow your character to act or behave in ways that are inconsistent with his character. This is called acting "out of character".

A good dramatist can project these rules into real life. If you know character, you can know real people, know what they are likely to do and not to do, and by so knowing you can analyze and project scenarios in real life. This can be a powerful tool in real life and in creating fictional drama. Either way, it requires a well-honed understanding of human nature and how human nature performs within the body and soul of different people according to their backgrounds, and their open agenda vis a vis their hidden agenda. Hidden Agenda's are fascinating, and the basis of suspense within an audience. The audience will know, ahead of your character, what is coming and has already figured out the plot to come, based on the hidden agenda of the hero and the hidden agenda of his antagonist, and this will cause the audience to root for the protagonist.

THE HIDDEN AGENDA-
OPEN SESAME

Everyone seems to have an Open Agenda and a Hidden Agenda. Look at yourself. The plans you make in your life and share with the world is your open agenda, and the plans you make in the hidden recesses of your own mind and often in the depths of your subconscious, represent your hidden agenda. That's not a bad thing. In the hands of a protagonist, his hidden agenda will be used for good, and in the hands of an antagonist, his hidden agenda will be malicious.

Looking at it dramaturgically, an Open Agenda would correspond to PLOT, and a Hidden Agenda would correspond to STORY. If our main character, a beautiful blonde, is in a room alone, having tea with someone whom the audience knows is a psychotic killer, and the audience understands that his hidden agenda is to kill beautiful blondes, the author will write the scene in terms of Text and Subtext, yin and yanging like a ping pong ball. When the psychotic inadvertently reveals his hidden agenda to the blonde, it becomes her hidden agenda to escape before he figures out that she knows his hidden agenda. But then, when he perceives her hidden agenda, the jig is up, so he pulls out a knife and she tries to get away from him. The emotional content of the yin and yanging of their hidden agendas, which is Story, has finally been physcialized by their open agendas, which is Plot.

See how it works. Text v. Subtext. Story v.Plot. Hidden v. Open Agendas. Yin v. Yang, constantly battling polarities creating dramatic tension. And you, as author, manipulating them with master strokes. Yes, you.

THE FATAL FLAW/
THE TRAGIC FLAW

It is said that the perfection of a diamond can only be perceived by the presence of its flaw. And so, perhaps, is the perfection of your hero perceived as he plays out his story. After all, Adam and Eve each had a taste for apples, and they were both the loser when Eve was banished from Paradise for having taken just one bite of the forbidden fruit. So, Eve lost Paradise, and Adam lost Eve. Paradise would never be the same.

For authors, Forbidden Fruit has come to symbolize that thing in the plot which a character with a Fatal Flaw wants so badly. When he or she desires forbidden fruit, the author has the basis for a story.

The FATAL FLAW comes in many forms, and differs from THE TRAGIC FLAW because The Fatal Flaw can , and will, be overcome by the main character , but The Tragic Flaw cannot be overcome. (See CAPE FEAR) The Tragic Flaw is inevitable. The audience knows that, and the character, Hamlet for example, senses it, does everything he can to avoid but the "tragedy" occurs despite his efforts to stop it.

If he is able to stop it, then it was merely a Fatal Flaw. In that case, the audience senses how dangerous the fatal flaw may be , but the character will either ignore it or play with it to see how far to the edge of tragic he can go. If he ignores it, it will catch up with him and he will have to deal with it...heroically, no doubt, in the end. Adam understood the Fatal Flaw , so he didn't eat the apple. Eve may have understood it, but she was compelled by her character and by her beckoning Fate to exercise her Tragic Flaw. Both had to abide by the Tragic Flaw , and so, we can deduce that , as a rule, the Fatal Flaw can be overcome, but the Tragic Flaw cannot.

As author, you may control your story by virtue of what dramatic weight to use and what direction you decide to take the Fatal Flaw as one of the tools in your Author Kit.

CINDERELLA
AND HANNIBAL LECHTER

Cinderella is so deprived that she dreams of having fun at the ball, but her gown will turn to rags and her horses and carriage into mice and a pumpkin at the stroke of midnight. And then to complicate matters, and , of course, to test her character, she loses her slipper as she runs out. But the Prince has seen her and tries the glass slipper on every lass in the land, and so, despite the flaw, she wins the day. (Thelma and Louise would groan!) She wins the day because of the way she handled her own Fatal Flaw. Her good character prevented her from trying to hide from the flaw; no, she abides by the rules...and she is rewarded in the end. After all, it's a fairy tale.

Thelma and Louise is a modern tragedy, because they were unable to overcome their Fatal Flaws, roughly translated as being female prisoners in a Man's World. Thelma and Louise couldn't overcome the disreality of the fairy tale promise society made to them as children.

And in an even grimmer reality of fictional life, Thomas Harris' characters in both of his novels, RED DRAGON and SILENCE OF THE LAMBS all have Fatal Flaws. Not just the antagonist, but the protagonist in each instance. Clarice Starling in SILENCE OF THE LAMBS and Wil Graham in RED DRAGON (made into the movie, THE MANHUNTER) have character flaws which almost precisely match the Fatal Flaws of the villains they are after. Yin and Yang. It is through the main character's understanding and introspection of his/her own Fatal Flaw that he/she is able to understand and ultimately catch the serial killer(s).

In the process, each of them puts their own life on the line, because in the end, his/her prey smells their fear, smells the fatal flaw of his hunter, and almost turns the tables on him/her. Thomas Harris, the author of the novels is represented in each of the stories by an evil and brilliant man, HANNIBAL LECHTER, more evil than the author for sure, but just as coldly objective and cunning, and just as perceptive of the fatal flaws attendant to the personae of both the hunter (protagonist) and the prey (antagonist.)   In this way, Thomas Harris has thrilled us with the combustible combination of Author/ Protagonist/ Antagonist/ Audience as a mirrored prism, all in one. How exciting. One man's flaw is another man's prey and vice-versa, around and around.

In the end, for us, it would be even more fascinating to learn what make this author, Thomas Harris, tick? What is it in his own character that returns him again and again to the same set of mirrors? Undoubtedly, he knows something about his own Fatal Flaw and uses it as the key element in his fiction. You too can do this if you introspect your own fatal flaw, how it has led you down certain paths, and how you have defeated the dragons in your life who would stand at the gate, ready to exploit your fatal flaws.

Between Cinderella and Hannibal Lechter lie the many choices you , as author, may make.

The flaw can be found and used by the author in many different ways. Blind Ambition is a flaw. Excessive Greed is a flaw. The feeling of being the "runt of the litter" is a flaw. Addictive Love is a flaw.

How and when should these flaws be used by you as an author? The answer blows in the winds of... your own character. I know you want examples, but that would just put you off the track. Each situation is different. That's why YOU get to be the author. You chose your main character, and he/she will reveal to you-- his/her flaw. You get to figure out how to use it to tell a story.

OVERLAY OF BASIC
INNER CONFLICT

You must establish the inner conflict of your character at the very onset of the story, and it will carry your story like the perfect wave for a surfer. Once you and your main character are on that wave, the ride becomes easy, ecstatic and satisfying when, despite the turbulence encountered along the way, you glide up on to the beach.

If, on the other hand, you don't get on that great wave, you will struggle from ripple to ripple, brave the current not to fall off, to make it through to the end.

Albert Camus' existentialist master novel, THE STRANGER, starts out with the first line, "Mother died today." And so, immediately, we FEEL the inner conflict of the main character. That's all it took. One three word sentence.

HONEYMOON IN VEGAS (1992) is a good comic example. Jack's inner conflict is blatantly and comically established in the very first scene with Jack and his dying mother, when she makes him promise that he will never marry, that no woman can replace his mother. Of course, in Freudian terms, this is the worst fear a man can have...and so, as the story unfolds, Jack's lack of commitment to his totally committed girl friend, allows her to wander into the shady hands of an older man who happens to be totally committed to the same things she wants out of life...marriage and family. Only problem is...she is blinded to the fact that this loving man is a rotten person and a ruthless gambler. Our hope, as the audience, is that Jack will wake up and resolve his inner conflict in time to slay his antagonist and win his damsel in distress.

The story is successful because, despite its shortcomings, it states the main character's inner conflict (fear of 'commitment' -in fact, it's been forbidden by his own mother) and the premise (what if?) what if a man who fears commitment to his girl friend, loses his girl to a man much more powerful than himself? His great weapon to be used as the REMEDY for his RESOLUTION at the end, i.e. LOVE CONQUERS ALL, and therefore his LOVE will give him the courage to resolve his inner conflict, whereupon he can vanquish his antagonist (the tough gangster) and win back his girl.

If you think in these emotional terms without allowing the plotting to get in your way, you will write successfully. Train your intuition to guide you along the lines of this kind of thinking, and you will always write successfully. If you do not think in these emotional and psychological terms, you will not write successfully.

ACTIVE V. PASSIVE CHARACTER

Probably the most common and most undermining fault in amateur fiction writing is the creation of a passive main character, instead of an active main character. Too often, the writer perceives his/her main character as a victim to whom things are happening; rather than a hero who makes things happen.

Your protagonist must always be an active character, capable of changing the circumstances around him through ACTION; you must take care to design him/her that way no matter what your own personal characteristics may be. Sure, it's okay if you create a victim, just so, as the story grows, so does your character ...and he/she will be moved to action no later than the beginning of the Second Act. Otherwise, all will be lost. You will lose your audience.

Speaking of the audience, the audience must from the very beginning perceive the seeds of an active character, even if, at the onset, the main character is victimized. (e.g. Thelma and Louise)

If your work is passive, you will not have a story, not one that works. Okay, so you cite BEING THERE, where Peter Sellers played a thoroughly passive character, and wherein the passivity of his character actually activated the world around him because people *mistakenly* misread his quiet nature as greatness. The comedy was based on his overstated passivity, and therefore it worked in reverse. Only proving that rules are made to be broken in the right circumstances.

What about RICK, the Humphrey Bogart character in CASABLANCA, you may ask? He just sits around, working hard to stay out of trouble. Thing is, you *feel* he has guts. He may throw you a curve, trying to get everyone around him to believe that he's only out for himself and won't lift a finger to do anything active. Metaphorically, he's like a cobra, sleeping in a coil in a corner ...but the potential to uncoil is clearly shown in his character. If he's not "passive", then he is "active", and the reason is that Active and Passive has nothing to do with the physical activity or the lack of physical activity. IT HAS TO DO WITH CHARACTER. Rick is an active, living character, and the other characters are reacting to him, bouncing off of his powerful persona. Rick is a thoroughly ACTIVE PROTAGONIST, and we know that he will inevitably do the right thing, actively make something happen to save the lives of other people. That he doesn't care or have much respect for himself does not make him passive.

What it does is make him a sympathetically REDEEMABLE CHARACTER.

THE REDEEMABLE CHARACTER

Your protagonist must have within his character the seeds for being either redeemed, reformed, or transformed. The raison d'être, the storyline, the theme, and the plot of CASABLANCA was singularly about the redemption of Rick. Okay, so he wasn't reformed or transformed... those are considerations for other characters in other stories. Willie Loman redeemed himself (in DEATH OF A SALESMAN) in a way we can sympathize with him even though we don't applaud him. Luke Skywalker never did anything wrong in his young life, unlike Rick, so he is not a candidate for redemption, he's a candidate though for transformation. He is moved to action by a righteous task and transformed personally in the process. In fact his transformation must precede the action he takes in order for it to be successful. He never heard of Freud, but Freud had heard about him...witness how Luke works out his Oedipal Complex, the fear of killing his father, and in uniting with Princess Laila, his fear of incest.

Yet, Luke, in his transformed persona, is a character we can believe in. Because, through The Force, Luke has come to know and depend on his intuition.

Intuition IS the Force.

ACT TWO

SCENE FIVE: PLOTTING

PLOTTING

BE A PLOT DETECTIVE

Phillip Marlowe and Sam Spade were fictional detectives, always involved in a good "plot." Now it's your turn. You can be a good Plot Detective, following the clues and finally deducing who killed who and what was his motive and how did he keep his wife from knowing and put the police on the wrong track, especially since we, the audience, knew all along who the killer was, and at the end it would seem that Sam Spade knew all along too...because he's plenty smart, he followed the clues even though we didn't know he was following them and there it is...the butler didn't do it. The author did it. That's you.

Yes, you did it. You're the author, aren't you? Aren't you the one who picked the killer from all the suspects, or did you know who did it all along? Sure, I know, you want me to teach you how to figure out a plot, how to invent the twists and turns and how to fool the audience, or the main character, and how to plant the clues, and when to make the whole thing "pay-off". Sure, you want me to teach you how, but I won't. Not only will I not, but I cannot teach it, because I cannot think for you.

I want you to think INTUITIVELY. I want you to "discover" the damn plot for yourself...it's there waiting for you discover it...in the character and the story. CHARACTER drives STORY...and together they drive the PLOT.

Part of your job as author is to figure out the plot.

This is hard work. The main thing to remember is that your task will be easier if you detect the plot instead of inventing the plot. The difference is vast. If you "invent" the plot, you will eventually get lost and fail. You need not forge the path. The path is there for you to discover. Discover the plot, don't invent it.

Remember. Writing is an act of discovery in itself. By writing you discover the unconscious hidden ideas and content you want to express. It is the same in composing music and in painting. It is just more obvious that a muse is required in those clearly non-literative disciplines.

And so, using the metaphor of Plot Detective will help you to overcome those fears of every creative writer; how the hell am I going to invent a plot to suit my purposes. Easy, Plot Detective. Be Inspector Clousot, or Ellery Queen, or Colombo; and in so being, you will invent the detective who, in turn, re-invents his author.

START WITH CHARACTER

Plot out the Story. Since Story is inert and unseen, it can only be revealed through plot. But for you the author, you may discover plot through the unseen elements of story and character. Start with character, and let character yield the story YOU, as author WANT TO TELL, not the story your character wants to tell. Your character will tell lies, but you will tell the truth. Your character, via his ego and his fears and his shame, will want to embellish, or change his story. He will fight you to tell these lies in the plot, so you must be in charge of this character, like a nurse's aid in charge of an Alzheimer's patient. Yes, it must be his story, not yours, but tell it your way, not his.

You are the psychiatrist who best understands your characters. In SILENCE OF THE LAMBS, Hannibal Lechter is an evil psychiatrist who is able to discover the plot for Jody Foster's character by combining his knowledge of the criminal mind with his analytical determination of Jody Foster's personality, and from this mind, guided by the author, comes the discovery of a diabolical plot, and its solution is "discovered", just in time of course, in the protagonist's logical understanding of the psycho's logical sequence of actions. The author is led by his characters, and they by him. It's the perfect detective plot.

So, Story is about love and hate, and fears and catharsis, leading to crisis, all of which results from the protagonist's actions. Let's say a story is about this man who loves a woman, who loves another man, or thinks she loves another man, and how he perceives that he must act in order to change her mind and her heart and finally falls in love with him. There's an entire story.

Now, through this 'story', you can seek out the plot? What does that involve? Follow the clues logically.

First, you ask yourself, (what does the protagonist want?) He wants X. Where can he get X? From the library? At the warehouse? No. From a woman. What kind of a woman? An old woman, a fat woman, an educated woman? No. From a woman appropriate to his age and circumstances and his upbringing. Why does he want a woman? Easy. Simple. Because he wants someone to love.

So, like God inventing Eve from Adam's rib, you, as author, can now invent this woman your protagonist needs as the counterpart to his needs...i.e. his story. He needs someone to love.

Now, you may consider the woman. This woman is part of the plot, not the story. The story must be the story of your main character, the protagonist. All other characters are part of the plot.

Now, inspecting THE INNER CONFLICT of your main character you can start determining, oops, ..discovering the conflict in the plot, i.e. the plot complication which acts as obstacle to the main character and as obstacles between the main character and the woman. You must have an antagonist. Perhaps the woman is the antagonist, who eventually is "defeated"., i.e. her resistance is overcome. Hm? Do you see how the antagonist can be subtle, represented by mere resistance, and not necessarily by a brute force. Starting with the basic Inner Conflict of the main character, the best choice is yet to be discovered. Perhaps the woman is resistant for a larger reason. The true antagonist is her father, who doesn't like the main character, he's not good enough for his daughter, and the main character must resolve his own feelings of inadequacy to show the father that he is indeed good enough.

Then again, perhaps his true antagonist is his own mother, who really wants him to marry X, rather than Y.

See how you are discovering these characters, not inventing them. How they are there to be discovered. And how the correct, the very best choice is to be discovered, starting with the basic inner conflict of your protagonist.

PLOTTING THROUGH TIME

Once you have the basic story, you can "plot" through time, i.e. the First, Second and Third Acts.

You have the basic story- man wants love, finds woman to love, must face obstacle to achieving love with that woman because, choose one- her father is against it, or his mother is against it, so he "loses" woman, then must (through Action of Second Act discover a remedy to use (in Act 3) to defeat his fear of her father, and/or his mother, in order to resolve his love for the woman at the end.

Technically, you know that good dramatic structure requires a Catalyst at the end of Act One. What should it be? You need a Catalyst. Hmm? What should it be? Well, guess what, it is not found by plotting out the First Act, but by acting upon the resolution of the Third Act. Surprise! Only by understanding the inevitable resolution of the story,...i.e. the main character wins the love of the object of his affections in the end, will you be able to understand what sort of catalyst is needed at the end of the First Act.

As author, you've discovered that the protagonist's mother is psychologically destroying him and his chances for happiness. You as author know it and you must find a plot device to reveal it to the audience. At the end of the First Act, then, just as he is about to propose marriage to this woman, his mother lies to her that her son has discovered her secret, that she is pregnant, and he will not marry her because he loves another woman and that he has left her forever; and then she lies to her son that his Love has run off with another man, and she sends her son, crushed, on a secret family mission to take over a company in Idaho.

Now, his inner conflict is greater than ever, he is betrayed by his mother, yet he still loves the woman he picked. The question now for us, the audience, is, does he have the strength of mind to discover the betrayal of his own mother, and the strength of character to take action once he learns the truth, through a series of plot devices you, as author, set along his path? That his love has had a baby, that it is HIS baby, that she still loves him, that his mother betrayed him.

And, of course, he does; and you help him through the plot to discover his epiphany at the end of Act Two, and you have allowed the audience to share the knowledge of the remedy, to confront his mother, find the letter in her bureau revealing where his true love has gone, and then...go to her, save her from some horrible fate she is about to experience, and let ...Love Conquer All.

Okay, now it's your turn.

STORY LOGIC

Story logic has to do with how things happen and when. Should it happen one way...or another? Should Sam Spade call on the Fat Man about the Falcon? No, logic dictates that it would be the Fat Man who calls on Sam Spade. Okay, then, at what point does Sam Spade become the active protagonist, taking action instead of receiving action? Answer...he acts when it counts, when his action can change the course of the dilemma from a negative to a positive.

Story logic traces, then, the path of the protagonist. What is "in character," and what is "out of character." Not just in or out of character, but in or out of character as it relates to any current situation, and then as it relates to the flow of the plot's dramatic structure. In the beginning, he will be in character to do one thing, and later he could be out of character to do that very same thing based on new events along the way.

Story logic is the forward logic that takes place as a result of the backward logic you have used to detect the plot as the Plot Detective. Above all, it must be logical. It must serve the story and not the plot. Therefore, you may take the plot on twists and turns which may seem to be illogical, but they are NOT STORY LOGIC, the logic of the unseen, which flows separately from the plot structure...but is served by the plot.

So, keep in mind that you are making the logic of the story, which is always constant, because it is simple, (he loves her, she doesn't love him, so he must find a way to win her heart.) Keep in mind the basic rules-- Character drives Story which dictates the Plot. This means that you must make the story logical before you are concerned with the plot. Your audience will know when it's not credible, when it's not plausible, and when it's out of character. If the audience doesn't buy what you're selling, you're in the trash heap.

ACT THREE

TECHNIQUES OF CRAFT

SCENE ONE:
TRICKS OF THE TRADE
CREDIBILITY, VERISIMILITUDE
AND DRAMATIC LICENSE

The essence of dramatic impact has to do with degrees of the intensity with which you use verisimilitude. Huh? What is verisimilitude?

IT IS THE CREATION OF A FICTION WHICH IS MINDFUL OF A TRUTH, FOR THE CREATION OF A LIE WHICH IS MINDFUL OF THAT TRUTH.

CREDIBILITY is that level of reality which the audience will accept without thinking about it twice. It differs from verisimilitude because it only asks the audience to suspend its disbelief. Verisimilitude IS fiction. Credibility is the suspension of disbelief. You need not ask the audience to "believe" what they see, only to accept its credibility.

DRAMATIC LICENSE is like "Poetic License." it is the author's privilege and a tool of his craft to be able to change true facts into fictional facts, for the sake of creating good drama. The audience accepts dramatic license and in fact, insists on it because the creation of catharsis is much more important to the audience than the creation of documented reality.

For the author, the restraints of Dramatic License, Verisimilitude and Credibility are tools for you to create dramatic structure and set the parameters of story logic according to the dramatic level at which you are writing. For example:

The power of The Force is appropriate in STAR WARS, but it would be ridiculous in DRIVING MISS DAISY.   Creating characters which are bigger than life is always the case, even in the smallest of dramas, but making Miss Daisy slightly larger than life is appropriate, just as making Darth Vadar extraordinarily much larger than life is appropriate to STAR WARS.

In a sense you choose the legend...if you want to make gritty drama, it is one thing to make a little story about Italian people in the Bronx, but if you want to make High Drama, epic drama so to speak, you will create characters that operate on a nearly mythological level. THE GODFATHER works on a mythological level. MEAN STREETS, on the other hand, is gritty and real. Then again, MOONSTRUCK is high comedy, nearly musical, nearly operatic. Each of these Italian-American Bronx story examples maintains verisimilitude within a context, and maintains it consistently throughout.

You, as author, have your choice of these levels. Like a menu on a computer, you must make your choice according to what you are trying to achieve, and you must examine that intent very carefully.

Once you have examined your own purpose for wanting your work to exist, and once you have examined it's inherent raison d'être (reason for being), and, after that, to what audience you choose to appeal, then you must work to decide at what level of verisimilitude, dramatic license, and credibility the work should operate.

So as to save the cost of making a period drama, the executives at Paramount Pictures wanted Francis Coppola to make a CONTEMPORARY gangster film out of THE GODFATHER, Mario Puzo's thinly veiled history of the Mafia in the United States. This was anathema to Coppola's dramatic purpose.

Coppola knew that his basic philosophical purpose, that factor which would present THE GODFATHER in a modern context was to "turn the myths in on themselves." To do that he needed an aura of mythological legend, both to examine the mistaken level of reality at which most audiences understood (the Mafia...and its mystique of Comorata (blood pacting), and to destroy that myth at the same time by showing that Italian-American gangsters are, at their core, just as middle class as anyone else. They love their families and seek to succeed in the world. GODFATHER as a period piece gave it other aspects, all of which reflected not so much on history, but **our lives now.** If you make the mistake of recreating history for the sole purpose of accuracy, you will not have made drama. Drama must relate to the audience at hand. The Mafia are not murderers in their own minds...they are following a path in order to fulfill their best hopes and aspirations for the future of their families. Blood runs hot in Latin cultures. Coppola knew this, and he knew he must create Legend.

Thank God he talked the studio into raising the budget from $4 million to $5 million. Was that the margin which elevated the grosses into the hundreds of millions of dollars? I think so.

Where and how do we use verisimilitude... how does it manifest itself? In simple terms, you make hate more hateful than it manifests itself in "real" life, and you make crime more vicious, and you make love more loving, you make a tall building even taller, and you make the difference between a tall man and a short man more pronounced in a comedy.....this is always the case, so it is the degree to which you do it which sets the level.

ACTION V. REACTION

ACTION IS PLOT.
REACTION IS STORY.

Each depends on the other for its existence, and the interplay between action and reaction create dramatic tension. In the movies, it is the hero's reaction which carries the story forward to the next piece of action in the plot.

The high point of the drama is a plotted event, on action, which produces reaction in the main character. ACTION is PLOT (i.e. physical). REACTION is STORY (i.e. emotional) A great example of this theory is the last scene in DEAD POET'S SOCIETY, when the boys, one by one, stand on their desks in honor of Robin William's' character, Mr. Keating, the maverick poetry teacher. As each one stands, and Keating reacts, the dramatic intensity builds, and it builds with the interplay of each boys' action, and Keating's reaction. It is musical, the beats and the spaces, where the spaces hold all the emotion in reaction to the beats. In the case of DEAD POET'S SOCIETY it will make you choke up every time, and it stands on its own. If you were to see it out of context, this scene would have the same effect. Somehow it represents the whole story.

And if you were to read it in the screenplay, you would choke up with emotion also, and so if you were to write it that way, it would be you the author who succeeded in producing an emotional response. And you would have done it because of your understanding of the relationship of action and reaction in building dramatic tension, either in a simple moment, a longer scene, or throughout the movie. Action v. Reaction is endemic to movies moreso than novels or plays.

You must always write On Action. It is a tool of your trade. Action is what carries the plot, which carries the story. Action is not the same as "activity", which has no purpose. Action is when an old child's sleigh is thrown into the furnace in CITIZEN KANE. Action is when the boys stand on the tables in DEAD POET'S SOCIETY. Action is when the headmaster walks into the classroom to see the boys standing on the desks, and his reaction tells the story. Action begets reaction which begets action, and together they create dramatic tension.

Writing 'on action' is not just the preserve of writing for the screen, but novels and plays as well. Just keep in mind that 'action' is Emotional, not Physical.

DRAMATIC PLOT -
STAY ON TRACK

The nature of a dramatic plot should stay on a track dealing with one major problem, and its solution. One and one only. Think about some examples.

The brilliance of THE MALTESE FALCON is its singularity of purpose for each of its primary characters...who will get the falcon? They're all after the falcon, and it resolves by sorting out the winners and losers. It might seem that there are too many characters with too many stories, but the fact is the problem is the same for each of them, and the resolution effects all of them, even though WE CARE about Sam Spade the most, because we identify with his character. And, of course, to repeat the primary truism of dramatic structure, the singular problem reflects the basic inner conflict of the main character. He is blocked from getting what he wants, and the block is in his character.

By examining your story and plot to make sure that it is singular in purpose, singular in the problem it must resolve, and that all of the characters are somehow related to the solution of the problem, is your task. And the problem is the problem of the main character, and the solution is his/her solution.

STAY "ON CONCEPT"

There are a number of elements to your story which could be considered to require staying "on concept". Premise, theme, story, plot, character, thrust and more. Which is the correct "concept" which best describes the message you intend to relate?

The answer is all of them, they are all what your story is "about." And, yes, it is important that your vision is clearly along one great path, which seems to be going somewhere important, somewhere we can believe in, and then, at the end, the importance of that "somewhere" is borne out, and the adventure is worth the ride.

What's the difference between staying "on track" with a singularity of purpose and staying "on concept"? Staying on track has to do with maintaining that singularity of purpose. Staying "on concept" has to do with weaving the colors in and around the main thread. The main thread is the embodiment of the primary idea represented by the protagonist's character. The main thread is the melody, and the threads weaving around it represent the thematic harmony, maintaining itself along the same bars and the same beat, as support.

Suppose you are Neil Simon planning out the story of THE ODD COUPLE, which was first a stage play, then a movie, then a TV series, and now, significantly, it is also literature, read as a play in schools and universities.

It's a good guess that Simon began with "character", a slobbish kind of guy he probably knew. He liked the character and felt he could work with it, that the inner conflict of a slob has enough substance to essay dramatically. Then he went about thinking "premise"--how to present this character in a conflicting set of circumstances.   "What if ..." a slobbish guy married a very tidy woman? No. Then it's the story about how a man resists being reformed by a woman. Not very appealing and leaving very little room for an active and sympathetic character. But, what if...what if...it's about two men, roommates, one a slob, the other fastidious... how they would get on each other's nerves like a married couple. Now it becomes A STORY ABOUT TWO GUYS GETTING ON EACH OTHER'S NERVES, a comical theme Simon has worked to advantage in other plays as well. THE SUNSHINE BOYS is the best example of the same sort of conflicts between two men who really care for each other as human beings, but don't know how to express it...because they are "men."

Now, we've got CHARACTER--a "slob" is enough for the central element of a main character. Add a little here, add a little there, give him specifics, but "slob" stands out. So when we add his foil...Mr. Fastidious...the conflict between the protagonist and his antagonist stands out.

PREMISE-   "What if..."...a slob and a Mr. Fastidious are forced to live together for the same reason? A-ha! They're BOTH going through divorces!--(THE SET-UP for Act One, Scene One.)

THEME- How men, who are rigid psychologically, act out their relationships and conflicts when they really don't know how to express their real feelings...that they are caring human beings.

RAISON D'ETRE- To express the theme that men who don't know how to express their caring feelings can find ways to express those feelings without surrendering their macho personas.

STORY- How two men with conflicting personalities can work out their differences, understand and resolve each one's inner conflict in such a way as to transform each other, and as a result, learn how to live more happily in the world of men and women.

CREATE, REPEAT, AND REPRISE THE THEME

See how the various elements seem to represent the same ideas, but with slightly different statements and plotting required. How, in a sense, they can each represent musical threads weaving separate colors through the same fabric at the same pace to create a rich whole cloth. How, over time, over the course of Three Acts, they will repeat and reprise, change their colors, heighten their values, add new threads in complementary colors as the story thrusts forward through its prescribed course of Catalyst, Catharsis, and Resolution. It does this around a main thread of singular strength running from beginning to end on a straight path.

The theme must stay its course, and as it does the audience will feel comfortable that you and they are on the same track. Perhaps a short tangent here and there for effect, but if the story starts out in New York City and the set and setting are New York City culture and it ends in New York City and not Sydney, Australia, you have stayed "on concept."

If you waver, try new themes and ideas in the middle of the story, or if you are not yourself clear as to what the theme and the premise and the story are "about", the story will flounder and end up on the proverbial rocks.

Know your characters, understand your singular idea, then create a clear path for the characters and the story to follow and you won't have to worry about staying "on concept".

K.I.S.S., Keep it simple, stupid. Your story will write itself.

THE SEAMS-
DON'T LET EM SHOW

The secrets of your craft belong to you, not to your audience, and certainly not to your critics.

Mark Twain opened THE ADVENTURES OF HUCKLEBERRY FINN with these words:

> *NOTICE*
> *Persons attempting to find a motive in this*
> *narrative will be prosecuted, persons attempting*
> *to find a moral in it will be banished; persons*
> *attempting to find a plot in it will be shot...*
> *..........BY ORDER OF THE AUTHOR.*

Oh, Mr Twain, you wily old coyote, what a nice trick. You don't claim that there is no "motive", that there is no "moral", that there is no "plot" in HUCKLEBERRY FINN, only that you don't want your audience to notice your tricks as an Author.

You changed your name from Sam to Mark and from Clemons to Twain for just that reason. "You" wanted to hide behind your authorship, and that's just what I advise my writing clients to do. Motive, Moral and Plot are for the author to know and use, and for his audience to enjoy without noticing the seams. When you see a man wearing a fine tailored suit, you don't look to see how it was made. That's the tailor's trick. If the seams showed, he'd have made a bad suit.

Yet, Mr. Twain, you have pulled off another good trick out of your author's bag by providing a warning to your audience. You, as author, have immediately made a heart to heart connection with the reader, your audience, and you hid that trick behind your caveat about motive, moral and plot.

So, Author, the secrets of your craft and your authorship belong to you and not to your audience and not to your critics. Don't show off your techniques. Hide them. Maintain the audience in a suspension of its disbelief by keeping the secrets to yourself.\

Hat's off...to you, Mr. Twain.

DRAMATIC V. LITERARY

How can you avoid creating a perfect structure and a perfectly crafted piece, derived on the surface from your main character's inner conflict, following all the rules, and it still turns out to be flat and uninspired? Perhaps it has the verisimilitude needed to being an inspired work, and yet it falls flat. God forbid that it appears to be great in the script stage, but falls flat on its face as a movie because, in the end, alas and alack, it is literary rather than dramatic, or theatrical instead of cinematic.

This has to do with the proscenium arch in theatre. It is that framework behind which the actors must stand and act out the drama. It is acceptable in theatre, and HEDDA GABBLER will have the audience's collective viscera wrenching from beginning to end. But then HEDDA GABBLER on film will lose us in its theatricality. OF MICE AND MEN is a great novel and despite great acting and a great story, in the end, we will not have had the visceral, gut-level CATHARSIS that comes with the movie experience. A novel too, in its literary quality, will have separated the audience and the drama by an invisible proscenium arch.

REACTION IS DRAMA

If you are writing a play or a novel, you need not heed this advice; but if you are writing a movie, you must beware this problem and avoid its pitfalls. How?

You avoid being literary and theatrical by creating a free flowing character in a free flowing story that observes the basic rules in a visceral context. Huh? What is a visceral context?

Firstly, you must write ON ACTION at all times. Even when you are writing literature rather than mere movies, you should write emotionally and when you write emotionally, you are automatically going to write On Action.

Secondly, you must value and give greater dramatic weight to ACTION and REACTION than you would in any other dramatic form. It is what HEDDA GABBLER has to say which is the drama of that play, and it is her husband's reaction which is the proof of HER drama. In the movies, it is the reactor and the reaction which carries the real drama. When Tom Cruise *reacts*, his wry smile is where the drama lies, that is the emotional content. When he acts out on the basis of his reaction, that is not the drama. That is the Action. Action and drama are not the same. Action is the vehicle to carry the drama, or to carry us to the drama, which is always the reaction. In the reaction is the emotion of the character, of the audience in response, and to the author who created that character to make a drama.

This may be why the movies tend towards heroic characters, because the medium demands the reaction of the main character; whereby in novels and plays, the reaction of the audience to the drama is the greater priority.

COLORS

Think only in Black and White terms, and fill in the colors later. That's how a landscape painter approaches his subject. He paints in the dominant blocks of images with shades of black, mixed with white, to produce a gray scale. he starts with the dominant areas in the foreground, then shades in the background in grays and whites...and when a satisfying overall "look" is accomplished, then he begins to paint in the colors.

You do the same. Know your bare-bones dominant elements, the main character, the main supporting characters, the place, the main story points, and think of them in shades of black and white. Your main character is good (white), his antagonist is bad (black)---but not all good and not all black, so add in the main counter balancing factors, the grays to give depth and story value to the characters. Paint in the main story points in black and white. Consider the priority of importance, where they will be placed in the landscape...and how small or large, in the foreground or the background.

Obviously, your catalyst and your epiphany will loom large, and so will the remedy and the resolution. First things first....don't plot out the whole painting. Show the Main elements first and then you will see where the plot can be placed, thinned or thickened.

This is the value of the One Page Idea, which then expands to the Three to Five Page Outline, and on to screenplay, novel or play.

PARALLEL CUTTING

As an author, you will always have two opposing forces at your technical disposal, represented by the dynamic yins and yangs of dramatic structure. In a scene, it will be two characters pitted against each other, striving to resolve their conflict with a payoff to the scene.

In the same way that the camera may cut back and forth between the two characters, starting with an establishing shot, and ending more dramatically, with Close Ups, you have at your disposal a basic overall technique called Parallel Cutting.

You build the tension of a movie through the use of parallel cutting from one scene to the next. In the broadest sense, you are cutting from the action of the protagonist as he works through his catharsis, trying to resolve his inner conflict and his outer conflict---to the action of the antagonist who is trying stop the protagonist from accomplishing his goals, especially if the goal of the protagonist is to "kill" the antagonist. In THELMA AND LOUISE, they are the protagonist trying to avoid the antagonist, represented by the Police Lieutenant, Hal; and eventually they must take a stand against the antagonists, which they do in a uniquely sad twist of plot and story.

Although parallel cutting is used more subtly to build dramatic tension in the First and Second Acts, it is pronounced in the Third Act when the story "cuts to the chase."

You can pace your story by the use of parallel cutting in the script. Simply enough, your scenes and sequences will be generally longer in the beginning, and will tighten up as the story gets tighter.

Read some scripts, novels, and plays by authors you respect to see how this technique is used. And then, when you outline your own story, try to pace the story with a sense of how long and how dramatic the intercutting between your scenes may be. There is no yardstick to measure it, just your own sense of pacing. Think like a symphonic composer, musically, creating tension through the interlink between melody and harmony, and the musical sense of dramatic tension you want to create.

DIALOGUE
"WHO ARE THESE GUYS?"
"TO BE OR NOT TO BE, THAT IS THE
QUESTION."
"CALL ME ISHMAEL"

People speak in layers of deceit; so it's what is not said which is more important than what is said. What IS said will ALWAYS be the window to the inner mind, inner fears, inner soul and inner truths... to a new layer of deceit and a new layer of truth, on and the same, which can then, again, be dissected.

Read Salinger, WAR AMONGST THE ESKIMOS, always dialogue hiding inner truths.

Dialogue... the less the better. Action speaks louder than words, and reaction speaks even louder... the effect an action of a piece of dialogue has on the person at issue. Let the cross currents sparkle AROUND the dialogue.

Hemingway said it's the spaces between the lines which tell the story, not what the characters actually say when they speak.

It is often stated that dialogue is useful in revealing character, but dialogue is the lowest form of action. In itself, it does not reveal character. It hides character, and clothes or reveals hidden agenda. It is the ACTION and REACTION surrounding dialogue that tells the story. Subtext of dialogue are the ideas and themes, you as author, want to reveal through the deceit that is dialogue.

In a play, dialogue is the basic dramatic content. In movies, the basic content is the action and reaction surrounding the dialogue. In novels, dialogue has another value attached to it, it is the writer's tool. The author can immediately explain the subtextual meaning of the dialogue by explaining the speaking character's inner thoughts and motivation. And this author can do this so continually that the Yin and Yang of Text and Subtext can be used as the basic structure of the novel. How well he uses this combination is the test of the novel's value.

In movie writing, the author is stuck in an odd spot. He knows that the dramatic weight of dialogue has a low priority when the movie is brought to the screen; he knows that "action" and "reaction" have the most dramatic weight in a movie; yet he's faced with an enigma---he's not writing a movie, per se, he's writing a screenplay to be read then translated into a movie by a collaboration of artists: producer, director, actors, cameraman, and editor.

In any of these three formats--novel, screenplay, and play--the purpose of dialogue is to deliver Text and Subtext. It is the percentage usage that makes the difference. In the novel, dialogue probably carries 90% Text, and the subtext is then added in complementary fashion by the author's explanation of the character's meaning. In the play, dialogue is probably 50% text and 50% subtext. The playwright knows he has almost no tool other than dialogue to convey his meaning through the continuity of Time. And, unfortunately for the playwright, and what makes plays his special province, he has no direct way to deliver subtext except by the interpretation of the reader, and then, the director, actors, and finally, the interpretative abilities of the audience. Dialogue must be delivered as Text, but understood as Subtext.

In the movies, the writer's trick is to write dialogue that serves well as both Text and Subtext in a subtle balance where it is perceived as Text, and even less than text, it is best delivered to convey dry information. The Master Scenarist knows that the Text is best delivered on the Action and Reaction going on around the dialogue. And surely, when it is ably brought to the screen by a collaboration of artists led by a great interpretative director, the dialogue will be subjugated and will only serve as an adjunct to the action and reaction going on around the dialogue. This is the ideal, and it is the task of the writer to "write" the action in such a succinct and focused, thematic way, that the reader will understand the subtext, and still enjoy the dialogue for it's textual value.

What is the "textual value" of dialogue. It is that dialogue that has no "Meaning". It is purely informational in it's ideal form, so much so, that when the Sundance Kid says, "Who are these guys!?", we gather so much information from that statement, that it's impact on the action is what becomes meaningful. This illustrates the value of Dramatic Weight. It is a piece of dialogue which has more dramatic weight than the author could have found by choosing some other tool to convey the subtextual meaning. Sundance is scared for the first time, and for the first time, he understands that the simple odds in favor of being an outlaw have changed. Notice, Sundance doesn't say, "I'm scared. Maybe this time, I'm not going to make it!"

No, he says, "Who *are* these guys?!"

DRAMATIC WEIGHT

In a scene, a character mentions that another character helped to fight a forest fire, and broke a leg going over a cliff.   Later, as the main character is strolling with his girlfriend on the avenue discussing their love affair, the character who broke his leg is seen across the street, hobbling along on crutches, with one leg in a cast.   They wave to each other and the two characters in the foreground, after commenting that the background character's ability to play tennis in this weekend's tournament has been scuttled, they go on discussing their love affair.

Now, in the above scenario, the character with the broken leg has been given little weight by comparison to the two main characters.   His story is ancillary to their story, and as audience, we give little dramatic weight to that character's story.   He is there for the convenience of the main story.   If his story eventually pays off, we can call it a "sub-plot."

But suppose, instead of his dramatic battle with the forest fire, and the breaking of his leg, being merely mentioned in dialogue, the author chose to show it. And instead of his being seen in passing across the street, he is seen on the same side of the street approaching the two main characters, and instead of their exchanging a wave from afar, they stop on the sidewalk and engage in conversation, and then as he goes, he trips over a lamp post and re-injures his leg?

Now, this character, and the story around him, has been given greater weight by the author.   It is the author's choice.   And as such, it is a powerful weapon in the author's arsenal.   Simply enough, in a play, more dialogue gives more wieght to a character.   And in a novel, more page space gives more weight to a character, a sub-plot, or any other story element.

When you are writing for film, dramatic weight has visual value, as well as sound values.   In THELMA AND LOUISE, the continual use of tractor trailer trucks, and other background noises, were used so subtly and so appropriately, that their cumulative effect became as a major character in the movie, underlining and pronouncing the theme. Vis-a-vis the simple story line, it helped to give meaning to what appeared superficially to be a standard "on the road", "against all odds" type of plot line. It was like a musical soundtrack, but better. Similarly, murals and landscapes were continually painted as back-drops, beauty interrupted by dirt and commerce, just as Thelma's and Louise's free spirits were continually assaulted in the simple plot lines. None of this was accidental, one must assume. In fact, these aspects were suggested by the author in her screenplay, and the director expanded upon the author's ideas. After all, movies are a collaboration of authors... writer, director, actors, cameraman, producer, wardrobe, make-up, art direction, etc... and your job as screenwriter is to provide the inspiration for each collaborator. It is a subtle test of your skills. You cannot spell it out visually, you can only suggest by the tone and texture of your words... what the tone and texture of the final film should be. And just as you are the author of the screenplay, you will be the author of the response of your collaborators. And one of your tools is DRAMATIC WEIGHT.

PYRAMIDING CHARACTERS

E.M. Forster in ASPECTS OF THE NOVEL, talks of ROUND CHARACTERS and FLAT CHARACTERS. Your main character is the most rounded, and the people closest to him, and his antagonist, are at the next tier of the pyramid, and so on. It is important to maintain the pyramid. Just because a minor character is interesting, doesn't mean that character should be rounded. Certainly, not so well rounded as the main character. Forster says "Only Round people are fit to perform tragically or heroically". Think of it this way, see if this works for you: Round characters are part of the STORY, and Flat characters are part of the PLOT.

METAPHOR

Metaphor is the single most important technique in the arts. It is most especially applied to writing. Again, it is a Greek word, so Aristotle probably invented the word, if not the technique.

Metaphor is your secret door to authorship. It should not be confused with symbolism. Symbolism is an up-front use of a symbolic object to explain or symbolize. Dreams use symbols to explain the secrets. A tooth falling out means death. Or, to a woman, a horse stands for a man, and if she is riding the horse, it stands for controlling a man. If the horse bucks and she falls off, it may be loss of control, etcetera and ad nauseam. Metaphor, on the other hand, is a tool for drama. "She's a fox. He's a pig."

When an actor does scene work, he often chooses a metaphor for his character. Fox, Pig, Mouse. Cat v. dog. Playing "cat and mouse" elicits an image which you, as author, can use to create the framework for a scene in which two characters are interacting, one slyly closing in on something and the other slyly, cleverly averting the other character, and the goals that character is trying to accomplish. Reduced to it's essence, they are playing "cat and mouse." And so it goes.

You can, if you like, offer this information to the reader, or you can simply use it for your own authorship. Use it as your own special secret technique... so when the reader or the viewer *feels* one character stalking the other, he won't know it, but he will *feel* that they are acting like "cat and mouse."

PREMISE

Premise is the basic idea for a story. Loosely translated, it is the "What if...?" What if a common man is chosen to be inspected by the aliens of a space craft from another planet? (CLOSE ENCOUNTERS OF THE THIRD KIND) What if two guys are forced by circumstances to live together, and one is extremely messy, and the other is neurotically tidy (THE ODD COUPLE)? What if a common girl is chosen by a gentleman to teach her to become a lady, and fool the gentleman's gentry friends, only to find that he falls in love with her (PYGMALION - MY FAIR LADY)?

Premise then, has been used for decades as the original basis for novels and plays, and more lately as the linchpin for TV formats, and often for episodes on TV shows, mostly comedies. Premise probably applies more to comedy than to drama or melodrama. Somehow, it has also found its way into the lexicon of film schools, and while premise maintains its place, as the launching pad of an idea, it is not so simple to identify the premise in modern movies, which so often base themselves on larger than life themes and mythological circumstances. Every good movie has a premise at its conceptual level, no matter what. What if the only one who has the power to kill an evil empire is the exiled son of its enslaved king? (STAR WARS.) What if... What if? The problem, however, with modern movies is that they often depend on premise at the expense of the story. When this happens, the Third Act becomes forced and often is predictable and flat.

SCOPE and DEPTH
BALANCING BACKGROUND & FOREGROUND

As author, you must decide on the size and depth of your canvas... what does it take to tell the story?

Too often the scope of a film, and even moreso for a play, will be dictated by its budget. Your task as author is to tailor the scope as dictated by the story, not the budget. CLEOPATRA ended up all foreground and million dollar scenes in the background on the screen for a few seconds at a time. Taylor and Burton held the stage, while the Roman Armies fought on the back-drop. Modern films have solved this problem by making characters so much larger than life that the background and the foreground become one. It is less than a solution for the screenwriter, who must find a way to suspend disbelief in the disbelievable. The solution has basically been to appeal to two dimensional audiences, basically children and imbeciles. Some very good filmmakers, Spielberg at the forefront, have taken this path.

What they do is use MYTH to create larger than life THEMES, and then the characters become nearly God-like. Simple ideas about simple people have little place in these MYTHICAL EPICS. The simple people become secondary, little people whose homey stories are subplots or sketch work. This has been a solution to the larger than life screen problem for decades, and with modern technology, sound systems, big screens, big budgets, it has reached its zenith, and there is nowhere to go. Luckily, HDTV is the solution, screens in the home, not too much larger than TV sets, but much smaller than a theatre screen.

For the writer, the task becomes more complicated than ever before. Keep in mind the composition, write for a 20 piece orchestra for HDTV, and an 80 piece orchestra for the Big Screen. How can a writer do this? By knowing his instrument is the entire orchestra. By using his String Section with all its power when he must, and by cutting it down when he plays for the hearts and minds of his audience. Let the director conduct this orchestra, choose the virtuoso, performers, etc., but give him a symphony he can conduct for the Hollywood Bowl. How? Okay, how?

In practical terms, by playing the big scenes and the little scenes off of each other, interspersing the drama to play character, story, foreground and background in a rhythmic pattern whereby the power of the little drama plays into and over the larger scenes. Coppola understood the need to do this when he wrote (before he directed) THE GODFATHER. He allowed character to be so powerful and to run the story that when the blood of the characters got so warm it had to run as bloodshed, the brutal scenes became smaller than they would have played otherwise. Smaller by comparison, by sharing the story with the little people dramas. In so doing, Coppola was able to even out the drama across a broad canvas.

And then, when Coppola made COTTON CLUB, he tried the same technique, but by copying himself, he was unable to maintain the balance, and so Background won the day. The background, singing and dancing at the Cotton Club, and the big scenes of brutality overran the the Foreground, the characters' stories. Their stories just weren't enough to carry the whole. How to fix it.

Screen Time. Give more screen time to the characters. Or even better, get rid of some characters, to increase the screentime for the more important characters. This increases the Foreground, as fewer characters fill the foreground, their individual importance increases. Soon enough the background and foreground are in balance.

THE STAKES

The Maltese Falcon, a statue, represented both the emotional and the physical stakes in both the novel and the movie of the same title. Tying the emotional and physical stakes together is much to be desired. Such a coincidence is rarely possible, but the closer you can come, the more closely your story will be tied to your plot, the more loosely the inner agenda of the main characters will match their outer agenda, the closer the inner conflict will be to the outer conflict, the closer action will be to reaction, and so on. If Greed is the catalytic agent of the story of The Maltese Falcon, and "greed is a cancer which eats one up from within" is the theme, then the Falcon stands as a far-reaching symbol of both the emotional stakes and the physical stakes. Whoever possesses The Falcon thinks he will be happy because he will have something beautiful and something to make him rich. Only Sam Spade has the inner character to know that happiness is built on something moral. He appears to be immoral, but it is always his morality which allows him to see other people for what they really are, and as a detective, to understand their motives via their character. Like a good author, or a good audience, he is always a step ahead of them.

And it is the towering symbolic presence of The Falcon which ties it all together graphically and cinematically.

PHYSICAL V. EMOTIONAL STAKES

Be careful not to invent physical stakes just for the sake of having "stakes" as part of your story. Just as you can have no plot without story, and vice versa, you cannot have physical stakes without emotional stakes. Sometimes it may seem that there are emotional stakes, but no physical symbol to match up, but this is not so. In THE GODFATHER, the physical stakes are a life and death issue, and the emotional stakes are POWER and the inner desire to maintain the survival of the Godfather, and therefore his entire family. But the emotional stake is the Survival of the Family.

In THELMA AND LOUISE, the physical stakes, again, are their physical survival against the cops who are after them (stemming from the plot), but the emotional stakes are harder to identify. My vote is--it's their self-worth. And how do you embody "self-worth" in a physical symbol? In THELMA AND LOUISE, I think it's embodied in the beautiful scenery, and finally the image and symbol of the Grand Canyon, that it represents something great about the human spirit and his connection with a spiritual realm. Conversely, all the ugly "man-made" machinery and activity all around them; the big truck, the noise, etc., was a physical symbol for that which they wanted to escape spiritually. Ultimately, then THELMA AND LOUISE is about the human spirit. That's how it overcame it's gritty political message about women in a man's world. What do YOU think?

How can Jack and Jill be imbued with emotional and physical stakes? From the little information we have, it can't, but give it a little story value; suppose Jack's intention when they get to the top of the hill is to give Jill a kiss... well then all sorts of things come into play, from Jack's Oedipal complex, to his reputation and Jill's reputation, and how the community will react, and then what does the pail of water symbolize?

RESEARCH
HOW TO   USE IT-- NOT ABUSE IT

If you write a story about Napoleon Bonaparte, you shall certainly require research. And, did you know that even if you do a story about a kid from your old neighborhood who just happens to resemble yourself and it's about an incident just one from your own childhood, you will still need to do research...even if it is scouring your memory for facts.

Research is collecting information useful to your story which will enhance the reality and viability of the setting, the circumstances, and surprise...your main character. When you create your main character, you give him a physicality and physical characteristics, patterns of behavior, and an "outer conflict" which will represent his inner conflict, and you eliminate those characteristics which are counterproductive to your purpose. You want the same benefits to accrue from your use of research.

Suppose you were assigned to write a story about a conflicted young symphonic composer whose need for recognition amongst the cultural and musical elite is so great that it's eating him up inside, in fact he is in denial, he **hates** the stuffy pretentious elite.

I was assigned such a story idea to write for Producer/Director Tony Bill and Warner Brothers in 1980.   Where to begin?   I had to create an assigned character out of whole cloth, and his story needed to be set in the rarefied atmosphere of the cultural literati of New York and set in a contemporary setting.   Okay, I had lived in New York, and I knew the exterior trappings of Lincoln Center, Carnegie Hall and the like. I knew one or two composers and had observed musicians....but not at the level I was to write about. Even so, I could "research" some aspects of the composer's personality from them, and, even better...I could "research" MYSELF.   Not unlike the way Stanislavski taught actors to "research" *themselves* in his book, AN ACTOR PREPARES.

I could recall the burning ambition that I had as a younger man to create great works and to be recognized for them by critics and professionals within my own chosen profession.   Like the character I was to create, I wanted to create not just good works, but great works, works which might change the world. But only on my own terms, sometimes a Fatal Flaw. Change the minds of the establishment, create a new art form. And so, in myself,   I found the burning inner conflict of my protagonist, and the Fatal Flaw he must overcome. But, I knew very little about classical symphonic music, only the stiff facts I had learned in a freshman year college Music Appreciation course, but I knew one important thing.....all the arts come from the same place in one's heart and soul, so that the musical heart would not be that different from the actor's or the writer's.

After that, it didn't take much to figure out that the world of the cultural elite is one of high social appurtenances, not cafe society, not wealth alone, but old money, the 400. The very, very rich...the establishment.

Without going to the library, I was doing "research", researching what I already knew about people and society to interpolate and blend into the story. To give substance to my main character, whose character would be more like a regular guy on the surface, just another struggling actor-type, and to find a base for his inner conflict in a typical psychological bind, I gave him a deep genealogy in the history of music....his great-great grandfather was a renowned Italian composer of the early 19th Century, and so were all his fathers before him...except that his own late father had failed to live up to the family name...and now our young hero's career was on the line bearing the burden of his father's failure and his ancestor's greatness before him.

For this, I really needed research, so I read up on the history of some Italian composers, found a family of Italian composers, and picked and chose and altered those facts to suit my story in fictional form.

I did the same for the Cultural Elite appearing on the other side of the story. The daughter of the Board of Trustees has a blueblood ancestry and is engaged to to marry the stuffy conductor of the Metropolitan Orchestra....but she falls in love with this disabled, disturbed genius on the brink of failure. I had known a few women of haughty upbringing, reflective of the main character, I characterized her on the other side of the coin, that she too had a burning desire to break from the bonds of her upbringing, and how she might be galvanized into action when she sees an injustice. This is "research" too.

With the basic conflicts in motion, a Theme emerged-- what are the consequences of Duty v. Love? The set and setting and the types and stereotypes of the story had to be meticulously rendered. I needed to make her fiance unappealing so that we would root for her to get rid of him, and so I made him a stuffed shirt, and , ultimately to be revealed in the last Act, a phony. Yet, he had to be a stuffed shirt with the education and credentials identifiable as part of the elitist swirl of symphonic society and fundraising.

So, unlike my main character, a middle class guy from Brooklyn belying his superb genealogy, I made the conductor a man hiding the basic roots of growing up in Detroit, Michigan and having cultivated a snobbish affectation of culture and art. The trick requiring research was how to make him a REAL fraud, rather than a transparent and synthetic fraud. Easy. I bought a book on classical music and allowed the character to pepper his speech with opinions and education that could not be disputed, but which were somehow not from his own heart. So, when his character is tested by our main character in a funny scene, he is humiliated and exposed and he falls apart at the seams.

Here's a short exchange from that screenplay titled IN "B"MINOR. See if you agree that it combines research with character so as to achieve a tastier story value:

(...continuing scene in lobby of Lincoln Center Music Center after a concert conducted by 'Eric Sattinger')

> CROWLEY WILLIG
> (eyeballing Sattinger)
> Dr. Sattinger....I have never
> heard a more inspired reading
> of "8" in B Minor...and I intend
> to say so in my review.

His outspoken committment is so unsettling that it takes a moment to break the pregnant pause, but Charlotte does it unwittingly as she joins the clique.

> CHARLOTTE
> Roll over, Beethoven...

> ALICE
> Char-lotte!

> ERIC
> Darling....

He gives Charlotte a dutiful kiss.

                    DEWITT
          Char, you know Crowley
          Willig....? Rog and Sarah
          Vanderheuven...

Charlotte nods politely. Sattinger looks at Willig...

                    SATTINGER
          Crowley...do you think har-
          monic inversion has ever been
          successfully used in modern times.

                    CROWLEY
          Scheidt used double counter-
          point in "Tabulartura Nova"
          and ... it worked.

                    SATTINGER
          In 1624!...and even then it was
          ....labored. I have never found
          way to make the technique flow.
          The musicians can't handle it.

Dewitt and Alice are intrigued.... listening to genius.
Charlotte floats away, and FOLLOWING HER past the two
fencing geniuses--

                    CROWLEY
          I'd like to see it done
          with voices...

                    SATTINGER
          Spectacular idea!
(cont.)

**Personally, I didn't know diddily about the
Tabulartura Nova or its interpretive implications. My
characters, however, knew all about it.**

So, I offer my own experience as an example of how research can be blended in with Character and Story. It must not stand alone, to show off the author's knowledge of the facts surrounding the Story. It must not surround the story, it must be absorbed by the characters and their story.

I was amused to see, when people who did not know me, read my screenplay, they were sure it had been written by someone intimately involved in the New York classical music scene.

....IT'S OWN REWARD!

Was IN "B" MINOR ever produced? No. A similar movie had already been put into production just as I finished the screenplay. Was I disappointed? Sure. But every written work stands on its own merits. It does not require a sale to a New York Publisher, or a Broadway opening, or a Hollywood production to be a valid piece of work.

For the Author, the process is its own reward. It is that which will separate him from a mere writer, looking to the market to put a value on his own self-esteem.

ACT THREE
SCENE TWO:

FINDING and FIXING
FAULTS

ANALYSIS:
FINDING AND FIXING
FLAWS IN "THELMA AND LOUISE"

At this writing (1993), THELMA AND LOUISE has established itself with an enduring place in the history of movies. It is a genre movie of two kinds. It is a "road picture" and it is an essay on the battle of the sexes, more political than its predecessors, the Capra film, IT HAPPENED ONE NIGHT, the Spencer Tracy- Katherine Hepburn classic, ADAMS RIB, and more recently, PRETTY WOMAN. Historically, in the simplest sense, the battle of the sexes revolved around women who were challenging men in a "man's world" and ultimately, when the heroine finally went out too far on her limb, she was rescued by her man, portrayed as a person who respects women and knows what's best for them. Ultimately, the woman agrees with that assessment of her place. In PRETTY WOMAN, the traditional double standard view of woman is inspected and reversed. The double standard is defined as a whore-Madonna syndrome where women are pigeon-holed as being either bad or good. The bad ones play around and are fair game for men, married or not, and the good ones don't play around, get married have children and go to heaven when they die, if they die. PRETTY WOMAN explores this myth, makes it self-destruct in the process of an honest relationship between two people who think they know who they are and what their roles are, but when the chips are down, each becomes a human being in their needs, and in a decidedly political-cultural twist, representative of changing times, he "rescues" her— and she "rescues" him "right back". As they are about to live happily ever after, some part of their roles will be traditional, but *emotionally* they will be equal.

THELMA AND LOUISE takes a radical cultural and political tack away from any of its historical forbearers. The author of the screenplay, a married woman named Callie Khouri, makes a very clever set of choices, which, without compromising her intent at any point, allows her idea to be embodied in a structure compatible with the vast audience required to attain commercial success. She made those choices with a practiced eye to attracting first a qualified and successful director and created roles to attract very successful, commercially oriented actresses. Basically, the design was to cloak a serious message in commercial garb, and still not be accused of wearing the emperor's new clothes.

The battle of the sexes historically has been fought in the movies in a sophisticated setting (including the office comedies, NINE TO FIVE and Mike Nichols' WORKING GIRL) in big cities with urban and urbane themes. Khouri made an essential decision as her first critical choice; she would adopt the franchise of a man's world to make a statement, i.e. she chose a male genre rather than a classic feminist genre, the "two buddy road picture." Once this was decided, other aspects of male genre came into play, put it "on wheels", put it in a western setting, a man's world if there ever was one, and make it a cops 'n' robbers film. Right then and there, without even knowing anything about the character of the two women, the context spoke for itself. Strong content before a word was written. Strong in story values, strong in commercial precedent.

Just think, rather than the story of two modern working women in a New York Hi-rise office building trying to escape their husbands for a weekend, it became two unsophisticated women in Arkansas. The imposition of Khouri's political agenda just became that much easier. It becomes SUBTEXT rather than TEXT, and now, in McLuhanesque terms, the medium becomes the message.

Take note now how clearly she was using her ideas, the conceptual part, and find ways to create set and setting, plot, and characters as the embodiment of ideas, and in ways whereby her ideas take on a life of their own.

It is this "life of their own" aspect which then allowed the author to bring her intuition into play, to allow the creative process, the muse, if you will, the alpha state, if you will, to take over, so that her characters could write the story through her as author. She could become the medium through which the story would tell itself. Mind you, she would trust her instinct to keep the plot in order, and as the story and the plot moved inexorably, thrustfully, on, she would make adjustments to both as she went along, and later, when she took a hard look at her first draft. I am guessing this was her process. As a result of this process, the thrust and flow of the story was so strong that it could overcome a number of technical flaws.

STRENGTH OF AUTHORSHIP
CAN OVERRIDE TECHNICAL FLAWS

And those technical flaws are one of the primary reasons I have chosen THELMA AND LOUISE as our working sample. It is said, aptly, I think, that the perfection in a "perfect" diamond can only be perceived by its flaw; and the metaphor suits the screenplay for THELMA AND LOUISE, whose many flaws are beautifully overwhelmed by the strength of authorship. Mind you, this authorship by the screenwriter also inspired the authorship of its director and its stars; given that the making of a film is known to be a collaborative process when its at it's best, that aura of authorship can first be traced to the screenwriter, and usually will be. So often, Hollywood movies are produced with the stamp of one person, outside of the collaborative process—i.e., the director, the star, even a deal making Hollywood agent or a studio, that when the authorship inspired by the writer carries over into the collaborative area with the director and the actors, the many technical flaws will readily be forgiven by that last part of the collaborative process, that intimate of the true author, i.e. the audience. It began with the Greeks, best understood by Aristotle, described as CATHARSIS... for all three, author, audience and the characters in the drama; and its truth bears fruit even in Hollywood Babylon.

What are the technical flaws in THELMA AND LOUISE? Okay, I will address the flaws first, and then address the techniques which serve to cancel out the flaws. The first flaw is that Khouri twisted the plot to serve her own purposes in a number of minor ways, and one major way. The major twist was, after Louise shoots the attempted rapist, Harlan, and they run... Thelma says they should go to the police, but Louise talks her out of it. Of course, Louise is in a panic, and these are two human beings who don't always think straight, and on top of that Khouri imposes a character point for Louise to explain away her decision... that somewhere in her background, something happened to her in Texas that would make her afraid to go to the police.

That something in Texas is hinted at throughout the film, and the more it is hinted at, and never finally explained, either in the script or on the screen, the more suspect it becomes as a plot manipulation. It feels imposed and it breaks a rule in that it is **constantly** explained away **verbally**, and never do we see or feel any graphic, dramatic, evidence of just what might have happened to Louise in Texas. Blatantly, it is the author's device. And even though a practiced eye can see the device and explain it, and an audience cannot, the audience felt it and knew it subconsciously. But, the audience also forgave it unconsciously as part of its desire to "suspend disbelief", and so the author got away with it because the overruling story-line was strong enough to submerge this flaw. Still, it is a flaw that could have been corrected and made the movie even better. And, in its correction, there is another flaw that could have been corrected at the same time.

"WHAT-HAPPENED-IN-TEXAS" FLAW

Before we offer a correction for the What-happened-in-Texas flaw, let's explore other possible directions to explain why Louise refuses to go to the police. Granted, subconsciously, and as part of the film's overall statement she doesn't trust the police because the police are men, and men can't be trusted. If she made just such a harsh and blanket statement, it would probably compromise her character, making her an overall man-basher, and a cop hater. But, getting down to the bedrock irrationality of why she won't go to the police suggests an answer to the quest. Okay, what happened in Texas? Here's an educated guess:

LOUISE WAS RAPED BY A COP! NOT ONLY THAT; BUT HE RAPED HER ON THE ROADSIDE WHEN HE WAS STOPPING HER FOR A ROUTINE TRAFFIC VIOLATION! NOT ONLY THAT; BUT HE STILL GAVE HER THE TICKET; AND FORCED HER TO APPEAR IN COURT, WHERE HE WINKED AT HER FROM THE WITNESS STAND, EVEN AS THE BRUISES ON HER FACE AND ARMS HAD NOT YET HEALED. NO SIR; LOUISE DOES NOT TRUST COPS; AND SHE DOESN'T TRUST JUDGES EITHER.

Okay, that's a overstated correction, but a tempered version can carry a long way in diffusing Thelma's early desire to kill the cops. Later in the story it would serve well again, and more than once. Suppose the cop who stops them for a ticket on the road is just that rape-worthy sort of cop that Louise fears. The incident where they arrest the cop and put him in the trunk of his own police car would be that much stronger, and would serve to help turn Thelma's attitude around as it does around the end of Act Two. Furthermore, it would render the gratuitous scene where they blow up the oil tanker truck of the foul-mouthed trucker unnecessary, and in turn that would allow more time (in a movie which was forced to leave some important ideas on the cutting room floor) to bulk up the story where it needs it. Can you see how there is an inter-connection of consequential corrections at play here? The correction of one problem can work to solve another.

AUTHOR'S PERSONAL FLAWS CREATE FLAWS IN STORY

Which brings us to one or two more flaws which are now easier to correct. These flaws exist in the PARALLEL SUB-STORIES about the Police Detective, only known as HAL in the screenplay, and played by Harvey Keitel in the film; as well as the general FBI agents and police characters around him, and the way they handle their jobs. Basically, here the flaws are not a matter of the author's weak decisions, but evidently by a weakness in the author's own personal character. She does not seem willing, or easily capable of portraying policemen, and possibly men in general, an overall weakness in the movie, accurately, or with compassion. What compassion she does allay to Hal seems imposed rather than heartfelt. Now, understand of course, that male writers have been accused for many years of being unable to portray women as they really are and as they really feel, so it is understandable that a female writer might make the same mistake in reverse; but it does not serve her purpose very well, and had she been aware of her own shortcoming, she could have easily corrected it, both by better research on how criminal investigators operate, and by imbuing Hal with a more well rounded character and greater credibility. It was also essential that Hal, on the other side of the PARALLEL PLOT CUTTING LINE should have been better plugged into the plight of the two women than he was. As it was, both in the screenplay, and the film, Hal was created to be the only thoroughly sympathetic male figure in the story. The problem is that the audience knew that, as it was firmly stated in dialogue and some elements of plot; but the author's audience (and assuredly, then, the author herself) never FELT it, because it was not firmly stated in action, story, and character. The give-away on this point was at the moment this character of Hal was meant to payoff; the moment when, at the Grand Canyon, he runs after them, a sole male among them, a sole male figure who tried, who cried out in their behalf, and his sad failure emblazoned across his face... does not work. Rather than feel his pain, we wonder about it, why does he care so much?

FIX THREE FOR THE PRICE OF ONE

It's too bad, because this flaw could have been, and should have been, corrected as early on as the Three Page Story Outline. The corrections are simple, but they must be made in three ways, one each in Story, Plot and Character. The correction in Character is that he needed to be established as a very caring cop; more caring than other cops. He could, for example, have been shown to be kind of a joke around the precinct halls. Oh, Hal's always taking up the cause for the girls. Is he just girl crazy, or did his own Mama play with his little dink when he was two? (laughter). Or, did he or his sister suffer molestation or abuse as a child, maybe he was incestuous with his sister and has worked to purge that sin all his life. It would be a question of balance, imbuing Hal's character with the right dosage of a credible fault to create him as a bigger, better mirrored-reflection for Thelma and Louise in their moments of truth. Second, Story — a correction in back-story which could work to advantage to correct not only Hal's credibility, but Louise's as well. As it stands, we don't know why Hal cares so much for their plight. That we have given him a characteristic of being a caring type of person, allows the author to fatten up his back-story to advantage. Suppose Hal and Louise know each other in some way. What if he were her long lost cousin, and what if he had abused her when she was a child? Too strong? Okay, suppose he was her first boy friend in high school and had committed date rape? Too strong, suppose he was her high school sweetheart, and looked on and did nothing when the football team gang-raped her? Or just suppose he liked her and wanted to be her boy friend in high school but was rejected; he still has a soft spot for her and can leaf through the yearbook for key memories. Now, he takes a special interest in her, so when he announces that "I know what happened to you in Texas", it's because he's tracked it down, and he shares a hint with the audience. No longer would Hal and Louise be disembodied voices at the other end of the phone lines, and his offers that they could come home and his efforts to clear their names would be more convincing to Louise... and when she refuses, we'll know it's mostly out of fear, and we can sympathize with her better. And, most importantly, the payoff at the end.., both for Thelma and Louise would be even more poignant because their final decision will have been made in the face of this very sympathetic rescuer having failed. Well, now it appears that in solving the story problem, we discover that the plot as it stands has become stronger and more credible and therefore does not need to be changed or much adjusted.

One final comment. When Hal becomes more real and more well rounded, we don't so much resent the one dimensional, cartoon values of the other cops, and, by the same token, the other men, big and small, from Darryl to the truck driver. By contrast, they have become supernumeraries. Also by contrast, the character of Harlan, the rapist, and J.D. the charming seducer-thief (of Louise's $6,000), and the historical figure, the cop who raped Louise in Texas, became heavier heavies, which in turn by contrast allows the good men in this drama, basically only Hal, and to some extent, Louise's commitment-shy boy friend, Jimmy, to become even more well rounded characters, and better foils to the bad guys. Yes, it's a question of delicate balance; and it is a balance that should be established as early as the Three Page Outline, after which the delicateness of the balance can be fine tuned in later stages, even after casting the roles.

There are other less notable flaws in THELMA AND LOUISE, but as long as the basic principle of the interconnective nature of correcting flaws is understood, we need not belabor the issue. Rather, let the larger point be made... that THELMA AND LOUISE works despite its flaws. Let's look at why and how:

POWERFUL CATALYST ENERGIZES STORY, PLOT AND ACTION

Aside from other considerations, some already stated above, THELMA AND LOUISE works because of the extraordinary impact of its one great catalytic event the attempted rape and the killing of the rapist by Louise. Rarely in the annals of films has such a First Act ender been so dramatically explosive that it, at the moment of its explosion combines every element of the author's tools and statement. It is political, yet personal, and yet again, universal. It combines the energy of plot, story, character, and action all in one. As a structural element it is quintessential. It is a movie event that understands its place in cinema history, and concurrently in the feminist movement. It reveals the anger of women at their dilemma in a man's world, and it reveals that without the cooperation of men, women may not be able to resolve their own dilemma, their strong feelings to the contrary. In this sense, the event foreshadows what is yet to come in the entire drama. It is destiny at work, and the inevitable ending is, albeit not yet revealed, a foregone conclusion. In and of itself, it has a powerful beginning, middle and end... and it gives notice to the audience of what this movie is about on an emotional and political level all at once. It is plot, it is story. It is character. And it is powerful. Powerful enough to obliterate all technical flaws.

After that, the story and the plot play themselves out like a ripple effect; and in the simplest terms. Dramatic form demands Catharsis and Resolution, and they come with a minimum of attention by the author. Thelma thinks they should call the cops, Louise doesn't. Thelma, despite being raped, is still without a personal constitution, so she remains vulnerable. Louise knows this and despite her best attempts to keep Thelma in line. Thelma is like Jello under the influence of a man. Louise plots their escape, but Thelma foils it when she lets Louise's money slip out of her grasp. This produces catharsis and catalyst for Thelma at the end of Act Two, when she takes matters and the law into her own hands, and they become hold-up men, uh, um, hold-up women. Now, in the denouement, beginning with Act Three, the plot seems to take over the story when tension builds as they run and the cops chase, getting closer and closer on their trail. In the midst of this plot-bound tension, Thelma and Louise begin to realize their own power and self-worth in a man's world. They become more and more free. Victimless crimes against property become their statement of personal freedom, even as they dig their own hole a little deeper with each step.

Finally, as the denouement unravels its last thread, they are caught between a rock, the cops, and a very hard place, the chasm of The Grand Canyon ahead of them. It is at that point that Epiphany takes place, their mutual realization that there can be no turning back. The remedy and the resolution come one behind the other.

As an audience, we feel satisfied. We have felt their catharsis and agree with the answer. We would do the same thing ourselves.

Simple truths, simple evocation of dramatic structure... all emanating from, and simple and easy because of the great catalytic event at the end of ACT I.

RE-WRITING-
THE SECOND TIME AROUND
WRITING IS FUN. RE-WRITING IS WORK.

Sad but true. Re-writing is the trademark of the professional. It's more like work because it requires analytical thinking and your good old intuition is no longer your best friend. You must depend on the Left Side of Your Brain, the side you hate. And you must work more with that brain than your heart.

You must be brutally frank with yourself, ready to destroy some good creative work, ready to humble a part of you that you were hiding behind in your real life. Take a good look and make a hard decision. Your favorite scene must go. In fact, the whole damn Second Act isn't working, but why?

Here's a tip. It's called:

CONSENSUS

Take stock. Have some people, even people whose opinion you might not value, read your work independently of each other, then see what each has to say about it. Watch closely for similar threads of feelings. Remember, most people are unable to critique in specific terms and the do not really know the rules of craft. If you know someone who does, give his or her opinion more weight, but don't discount the amateurs. They do know how they FEEL about it...and if they don't "like" your main character....they may not be able to say just why. But, if a consensus seems to be forming, don't fight it. Go with the flow....right back to the drawing board.

MAKE A CHECKLIST, AND CHECK IT AGAIN

Give the Cannon Planagram a try, using it as a checklist. What item on the list is working.....and what isn't. What interplays with something else, but because of that, cause and effect, the denoument has lost its thrust, slowed down when it should be unravelling quickly. Maybe the main character is passive, a Cardinal Sin, a victim instead of an active hero who will ultimately find a way to remedy his dilemma in the end.

Maybe the conflict is too small for your canvas. You're trying to write an epic with the tools for a short story. The list of possibilities is endless, but you will have to sort them out and then.....do something you thought you had left behind you:

THE OUTLINE- ONE TO FIVE PAGES

Go through the original process again. Write a one page outline, think it over, then write it again. Do it intuitively now, writing it in one quick session. See how well the new ideas blend with the old, what should be eliminated and what gains new dramatic weight as it fills the void, what seems to shift to another Act or scene, what characters survive and in what configuration. Try to turn ideas into story values and then see how your characters are acting and reacting to the news.

Take notes, analyze, pick and choose, then do it again. Write a longer outline, or even a Step Outline (sketching scene by scene). Write it once, twice, see if the changes are significant and whether it "works". Is it dramatic?...or dragging? Is it overcomplicated, or does the story work in **simple emotional terms.** Did you write it in emotional terms first, and let the plot fall into place around the character(s) and the story?

If so, then hopefully, you're ready to "fix it."

FIX IT

Don't try to fix everything at once. You'll put too much pressure on yourself. Fix it in stages. Fix one problem, and then see how it impacts other areas. Eliminate some dialogue. Suddenly, what was overladen is now light and airy and some of the holes you have made in the story line have added to the mystery. You've let the audience in!

Yes....don't forget your audience, put yourself in their shoes. Are they rooting or snooting or are they snoring away? Give 'em something to root for. Figure out how they are going to feel satisfied when they finish reading, viewing or playgoing. Play with them, keep em guessing a little, keep yourself guessing a little too. Remember, the story is inevitable, but the plot can twist around like a red licorice stick. Make sure your main character is alive. Living. Breathing. Fearing. Loving. Hating. Being. Human. Human being.

CHEMISTRY

Something is still missing but you don't know what it is. Ten to one, it has something to do with a human emotion. And then, when you have that emotional motor running, going through the gears, first, second, third,....then sock it to em! Sock it to em!

That's the CATALYST. Check it for placement. At the end of Act One, is there a chemical reaction between the emotion of the main character's story and an external dramatic event which suddenly launches the story into a new dimension (a Crisis) that no one could quite predict? Check the catalyst for dramatic weight. Is it too light? Do you have a whimper when you need a bang, or just a bang when you need an atomic bomb?

Is your structure sound? Ten to one the problem(s) go back to the outline. Something wasn't working, and you tried to force the issue. Check out your original outline. Are you sure it works? Yes. Well, then why is the love connection between the two lovers so damned boring?

DIAGNOSIS IS HARD, REPAIR IS EASY

Once you've diagnosed the problem, the repair will flow like a bulging river whose dam has been opened. You'll see.

NOTHING WRITTEN IN STONE

Your work isn't written in stone. It's written on paper, and there's plenty of that...to write and re-write, and don't worry, you can throw something out, and then put it back later. You can try three different endings and see which one works best.

CLARITY

Nothing tests better than clarity. Watch for mixed metaphors and confusing characters and actions out of character. Watch for overwritten dialogue and overwritten scenes. Clarity usually comes in small packages. That's why a short outline is your best guide, the shorter the better to look for flaws, to checklist crafty guidelines. Remember, when a scene or a script or a speech gets long, it probably ends up unclear. If you must overwrite to be creative, then do it; but go back later and weed it out...find the moments, the meanings, the essences, and let go of the frills.

OUTLINE AGAIN

When you think you've finished your whole opus magnus...screenplay, novel, play---then test it with a brand new story outline. Then, write a critical review of your work, including a reviewer's precis of the story.

Then see if the review and the actual work match up. Don't be disappointed to learn that it still has a ways to go. That's typical for the greatest authors of all time. Be encouraged. You're in the company of Hemingway.

Just don't kill yourself out of frustration. Write instead.

ACT THREE
SCENE THREE:

METHODOLOGY &
HOW-TO'S

WRITE FAST;
THE FASTER THE BETTER

The faster you write, the better you write.

Did you know that?

Know it now.

Do it.

Write as fast as you can, and you will get in touch with the Muse, you will allow your characters to simply use you as their vehicle, and you will see the most amazing results.

Not just for your short outlines when you sit down for an hour and write as fast as you can, look at the work, think about it for a while, and then write it again, and wow...it's better.

Even writing an entire screenplay or a novel or a play very fast, at least for the First Draft...start at the beginning and get to the end as fast as your fingers can fly on the keys. Don't get stuck, you can change it later, don't get stuck, you can change it later, don't get stuck, don't get stuck. Got it. Good.

Okay, now start writing as fast as you can, let your writing go faster than your brain, because you are an idiot...the "you" that wants to be deliberate, wants to choose and pick and hide the secrets when you as author must allow the secrets to present them to you...on the page, front and center...get em out there. Salute. Okay, I agree, say you...and keep on going, let the damn secrets provide you with the basis, the heart and soul of your authorship.

Don't "write". Just let the play begin.

Do it. Now.

ON FORM - K.I.S.S.
(Keep It Simple, Stupid)

Louis Sullivan, the father of modern architecture, said that "Form follows function". And with this one sweeping statement he was able to sweep away all the rococco embellishments of architectural style that had built up for twenty centuries. This left us with clean, easy lines of design as the receptacle for greater and greater advances in technology, not only in architecture, but in every form of design, including screenplays.

Form in screenplays consists of only four elements: Scene Headlines, Description of action, Dialogue, and Camera directions. Simply enough, Scene headlines are IN CAPS, Camera directions are IN CAPS. Description of Action is written in narrative form of paragraphs spanning from the extreme left margin to the extreme right margin. Dialogue is indented and under the name of the character speaking, IN CAPS. (Descriptive breaks and pauses in a single span of dialogue should be written on a separate line, indented and in parentheses.) If a scene is broken at the end of a page, CONTINUED should be written at the bottom of the page and again at the top of the next page. If you break in the middle of a character's dialogue, write (MORE) under the dialogue at the break, then re-write the character's name over his dialogue on the following page and under the name of the character, write (CONT'D).

Doing any more than this, numbering scenes for example, is beyond the duty of the screenwriter, and in the way of the reader. You are not writing a Shooting Script, you are writing a play, a Screenplay. Make the most efficient and inconspicuous choices that you can. Elaborate form will not impress a professional reader, good screenwriting will. Remember, Let Form follow Function. It is the modern way.

Try the following two scenes for sizes.

FADE IN:

INT. THE AUTHOR'S INNER SANCTUARY-NIGHT

OUR VIEW MOVES IN, OUR Author, beads of sweat on his brow, as he ponders the blank page on his word processors monitor screen. A bundle of nerves, he rubs his fingers through his hair with one hand, while he lifts his grubby coffee cup with the other, but just as it reaches his lips, he mumbles something, quickly puts down the cup and stretches his fingers over the keyboard, leaning in, ready to type. He stops. Hold. Hold.

                    THE AUTHOR
                 Damn! Damn!

Depressed, he retracts his fingers and sinks his head in his hands. Hold, then PULLING BACK-

A SHADOW begins to fall over his back. WE can't make out it's shape and then we do... it's the shadow of a woman-- lifting a meat cleaver above her head. And PULLING BACK MORE TO REVEAL-

It's his wife, CLAUDIA... as she raises the cleaver and is about to bring it down upon the Author's head. Trembling, she raises it high, and then she begins to shake uncontrollably, and as she does, The Author, still unaware of her presence, suddenly raises his head from his hands, and gestures triumphantly into the air.

                    THE AUTHOR
              That's it! That's it!

Excitedly, he begins to type, madly, with the inspiration of a concert pianist.

Claudia is still trembling uncontrollably with the meat cleaver above her head. She seems to be shaken in her resolve by The Author's new found eureka. It takes everything she has to stop the cleaver, but she does. She turns, and with a disconsolate and confused expression, she walks OUT OF FRAME.

The Author, left alone now, suddenly stops typing, hits his forehead with the palm of one hand, and resumes his most depressed position... head in hands.

                    THE AUTHOR
          Damn. Oh, no. Damn it.

We HEAR a door slam shut in the b.g., but he doesn't as we,

     CUT TO:

The above scene was written as an example of FORM, but it also serves as a sample of scene writing. Notice how it tells a story, self-contained in and of itself, but it also suggests that it is part of a larger story about The Author, his inner conflict, and how his inner conflict plays upon the person who loves him most. It is also tricky and ironic; that The Author is the author of this scene and understands himself and his fictional wife, understands that she would like to kill him because of his writers block, and that somehow he seems to revel in it. How about you?

MORE FORM

As you can see above, form must always serve your intent in the scene, and form must never alter your best intention just because you cannot figure out a form for your words and images.

Notice how the example creates character, story, plot, and images all at once. At your disposal is sight, sound, action of characters, cinematic theatricality (the shadow, shaking and raising the cleaver). This scene is fairly well written and offers stage and camera direction more than you ordinarily would. It comes dangerously close to usurping the director's functions but when it is written to produce dramatic effect in a cinematic way, a way which helps to produce graphic rather than dialogue expression, it will be understood by the director as a help, rather than a hindrance.

Notice how little dialogue there is in this scene, and even what little dialogue there is isn't really needed. It is more a concession to the medium of talking pictures than a requirement.

Note also, that if this were a scene in a play, it could be written almost exactly the same way, even the effect of the shadow is a stage available effect. It is only a matter of eliminating camera directions, and adding stage directions.

Although the sample scene above utilizes an abundance of technical form, okay within the intent of the scene, ordinarily, you must keep the technical form as simple as possible.

TECHNICAL FORM

A scene takes place either outside or inside, therefore you begin with EXT. (exterior) or INT.(interior) followed by THE PLACE OF ACTION (e.g. EXT. ESTABLISHING, THE MANSION or INT. THE AUTHOR'S STUDY) and then by either NIGHT of DAY. Technically, and historically, these are directions for the Production Manager so that he or she can plan by location and night and day, but when you are writing, they become the reader's introduction to the scene.

If you want it to be raining and the street lights are glistening their reflections off of the asphalt streets, simply then write the following:

EXT. THE STREETS OUTSIDE THE MANSION-NIGHT

It is RAINING and the street lights are glistening their reflections off of the asphalt streets, creating a dreamy effect. OUR VIEW ADJUSTS to discover WALDO sitting on a park bench, allowing himself to be drenched. He is intent on watching SOMETHING OFF CAMERA.

CLOSE ON HIS EYES, following something, but what?

It is Dana, protected beneath a large black umbrella and walking as fast as she can towards the big house.

Waldo gets up, follows several steps behind her.

The big house looms large as she approaches. A light goes on the third floor. Dana hears the footsteps behind her and turns, but Waldo escapes her gaze with a quick move behind the stone gatepost.

Dana turns back towards the house. Perhaps she imagined the sound of the footsteps. She moves quickly up the great stone steps... and as she approaches, the front door of the house opens as if by magic; there is no one there. She glides quickly though the door, hesitating to close her umbrella and take a quick look into the void. She disappears through the great door, which closes mysteriously behind her.

From behind the stone gatepost, Waldo appears, staring at the house and looking up, he sees—

The light in the third floor window takes on Dana's silhouette, moving back and forth... and then she disappears one last time, and the light goes off.

Waldo turns. His brow is furled. He takes a deep breath, turns and walks away, leaving but his long shadow in the glistening reflection of the street lights on the rain soaked street.

CUT TO:

Notice how many different CUT TO's and CLOSE-UP directions The Author might have used in the above scene, but in the end he left all of that up the director's discretion. Yet the scene has cinematic life. We can almost guess when the director will choose a Close Up, or when he might cut from one person to the other. If you remain as a writer during the actual production, he may even ask you to create a SHOT BREAKDOWN for this scene. But he doesn't need you for this task. Remember, this is a collaborative art form, and this is his task, and he can design the shot sequence himself, and will likely do so in consultation with his cameraman, lighting director, sound man, and even with his film editor, to determine pacing, and how he might use close-ups and camera angles for dramatic effect.

As author, you will be satisfied to know that you provided the director and his creative staff with words that make the scene live and breath and suggest it's flavor through the dramatic action which you have created on the page.

DISSOLVE SLOWLY TO:

CAMERA DIRECTIONS

Camera directions derive from two points of view, the audiences point of view, and a character's point of view. The audiences point of view can be expressed as "OUR VIEW:, e.g.: OUR VIEW MOVIES IN, OUR VIEW PULLS BACK, OUR VIEW TRACKS ALONG WITH, OUR VIEW RISES ABOVE THE TREES, etc. A character's point of view may be expressed as JOHN'S POV: He sees Karen running away, etc. The use of a technical camera direction for John's point of view should be reserved for very specific dramatic effect; it will usually be assumed that it is from his point of view. In most cases, it is the director's choice. So, save that camera direction for those times when you insist that it be your choice as author, and of course, your reason for doing so must be sound.

Most importantly, try not to use camera directions in a stilted way. Let them go with the flow of dramatic writing, part and parcel.

Read some screenplays for Form and other good reasons.

FORM IN NOVELS

There is no form for novels. You're home free from beginning to end. You want Chapters, fine, write chapters. You want to be James Joyce or Jack Kerouac. Who needs chapters. Write any length on a roll of shelving paper. You make form, you don't have to follow form. Read some novels for Form and other good reasons.

FORM IN PLAYS

OK, so you need some stage directions here and there. Say what the actors are wearing, and the set and the setting . You need to time it...somewhere between ten minutes and ten hours (Remember NICHOLAS NICKLEBY?).

You can have as many Acts as you desire, but don't forget classical structure demands Three Acts even if they are imaginary and invisible at the seams. Beginning, middle and End. Read some plays for form and other good reasons.

STEPS IN THE PROCESS

THE ONE PAGE STORY IDEA-
One page, communicative, so it can be read and discussed with others

THE 3 TO 5 PAGE STORY OUTLINE-
Three to five pages written in one sitting, with beginning, middle and end, exposition, catalyst, catharsis, remedy and resolution. All... On Action! Do not plot it out, just show main points.

OPTIONAL TREATMENT OR STEP OUTLINE-
Sketching out the scenes, planagramming, or any method that suits you... this is essentially note taking for your own purposes, not to discuss with others.

SUPERFAST ROUGH FIRST DRAFT-
SEVEN TO TEN DAYS- YOU CAN DO IT
UNDER 110 PAGES- Write this as fast as you can in seven to ten days. Do not get stuck. If you have written something in scene 10 which does not jive with what you're now writing later down the road, figure on fixing the earlier part of the script after you're finished, and just stay on track, chugging away until you get to your final destination. The important thing is to get to the final destination, and if along the way, your vehicle has suffered dents and scrapes, a lost fender, and the engine is steaming and over-heated, don't worry about it, you can fix that later. Enjoy having reached your goal.

SECOND DRAFTING
This is where you become a professional, willing to be ruthless, throwing out your favorite scenes, lines of dialogue etc., and straightening out the story, creating consistency of purpose, adding and subtracting. This requires note taking, lots of thought, sleeping on it, allowing your alpha state to churn, then, if you're brave, you'll throw out the first draft, and write an entirely new draft from beginning to end. If you're not brave,

and the first draft was in pretty good shape, you can cut and paste and fix the first draft. Make sure that you fix whatever flaws were overlooked in the story outline, and have become glaring. Use your checklist, the Planagram. Watch your ego. Make sure you don't love it too much.... because it can definitely get better.

THE ONE PAGE IDEA AGAIN

The purpose of the one page idea is to discover your own thoughts and to see what basic organization you first gave those thoughts.

Hopefully, the core of your idea will appear as a focal point. You can then use that to build on. Sometimes, the main character will become so pronounced that we know that is what your story will be about. Additionally, your personality will be revealed in some way or another, and your artistic temperament. You will need a sounding board for that one page idea... someone you respect to ask critical questions. Simple questions: What is the story (emotional)? Who is the main character? What does that character want? What is his/her inner struggle? Is there a sense of events bringing change to the main character? And, even more important, how does the main character behave in such a way as to impact the story and bring about change? What is the final resolution of the story? None of the answers need be spelled out, and none of the story need to be described in terms of PLOT; except as plot and circumstances impact the story for our understanding. If it takes place in post Civil War, Atlanta, that would be important to know.

Typically, the first draft of the One Page Idea will be flawed. And it will be flawed, not by what IS there, but by what isn't there. Often, an inexperienced writer will presume that the reader knows or understands about what isn't there. This is a major mistake, and it is a fault in the author that he/she must continually monitor... "Am I presuming that the reader knows something that I have therefore neglected to write?" The reader only knows what he can read. Certainly, if the setting is Atlanta in 1867, he can presume certain things. But the reader is not a mind reader... he can only read what's on the page. Amongst my students, those who make these types of presumption are always shocked to learn that the reader didn't know something the writer presumed they would.

The argument that you can't write everything in a one page idea is completely false. Words are powerful, and the efficient use of words of power will convey the sense of things unwritten. The order in which the idea is organized will convey a sense of whether the author is thinking clearly, and whether the author's story will be understood.

But take heart. The purpose of the one page idea is so that the very essence of your idea can be analyzed, and with the knowledge of the analysis, you have the opportunity, in short order to rewrite the one page idea again. And again. And again. Remember that the greatest value of writing down what you are thinking is to discover what you are thinking. Each time you write, you tug and pull a little more from your subconscious mind into the realm of your conscious mind. It is your dreams. Let it flow.

And when you are finally able to make sense of it on the conscious level, you will be able to inform your subconscious level of your intentions.

To illustrate the process, I suddenly ask each of my students before they even begin, "Quick, in one or two sentences, what is your idea for your story? Don't think about it. Just blurt it out." If the student starts by saying it's "The story of a man who...", then I know he is on the right track... because it's about somebody. If he tells me, "It's the story of how the Guadacanal Islands were captured in World War Two," and he doesn't quickly follow with something about the main character, I know that he has an amorphous idea that needs to be focused. The focus will be the main character, and I will want to know something about that main character. If he/she tells the story in terms of plot, I know he's in trouble. If he tells it in terms of emotional dilemma, no matter what the plot, I know he's got a grip on his idea, ...at least to begin.

QUICK, WHAT'S YOUR STORY?

When I asked a new student named Greg,   "..... quick what's your story?"
 He said:

"It's about a guy struggling with right and wrong. He thinks he knows what the right thing is to do, but gets wrapped up in trying to appease other people... before he eventually struggles to the right thing."
Good start, because Greg started with the emotional and moral issues confronting his protagonist rather than hiding the emotional issues behind "plot". Then I asked Greg about the plot, and he said, "It takes place in the realm of auto insurance, fraud, bodily injury. I used to be a claims adjuster." Now, putting "story" and "plot" together we immediately knew just about everything we needed to know about Greg's story. Now, he has a "quick pitch" for his story, something like this:

```
It's about an auto insurance adjuster
faced with a moral dilemma when he's put in a
compromising position trying to appease his
friends in a fraudulent claim.   He must
struggle with right and wrong, and through
the help of his girl friend, he is able to
finally do the right thing.
```

The "girl friend" was suggested by Jody, another workshop member, and she was right... instinctively Jody knew that Greg's protagonist's moral dilemma could not be worked out by himself. The protagonist needed someone to embody the inner voice of his conscience. The girl friend could be his Jimminy Cricket.
What was most interesting about Jody's apt observation for Greg's story was that she was not that capable of seeing her own problems with "story". Instinctively, however, she found an element that Greg needed. Then, it becomes Greg's problem of how to see the answer before the question was even asked. And so

it goes. With experience we can learn to eliminate these problems as the rules in applying the creative process becomes understood. Like learning to drive a car; at first, we're all thumbs. If we learn well, however, driving becomes second nature. And so will writing creatively.

Now, in the next phase, Greg could add a few plot details about the man, the fraudulent scheme, and his girl friend.

At that point, he will have a very successful one page idea, and after some thought, note taking, and perhaps an exchange of ideas with a teacher or a friend, he'd be ready to start in on his three to five page outline.

Unfortunately, or perhaps fortunately, I felt duty bound to inform Greg that the arena of auto insurance fraud is a subject much in the news, and it was a very good bet that several stories on this subject were already being developed in Hollywood, and since Greg's screenplay would be on speculation, he would be one sad young man if he were just putting the finishing touches on his screenplay after six months as a labor of love, when a Hollywood studio announces a similar plot going into production. I knew this from experience!

I pointed out to Greg, however, that his story (i.e. .: the man in a moral dilemma) would always be valid, and he could simply apply it to another milieu. Let's see, how about Corporate Fraud as it applies to the environment? Vaguely in the news, but not so current. If not that, something else. Remember, plot in and of itself is dead weight. It only has value when the emotionally of "story" is breathed into it.

Despite my caveat, Greg felt strongly about the arena of Insurance Fraud...and we were both right! I was right that his story was strong enough to apply to any arena, and he was right because the strength of his story, as it evolved, was such that it diminished the arena's importance to the story. He took the risk, and I supported him. It's a risk every step of the way anyway.

ONE PAGE STORY IDEA - FIRST TRY
THELMA AND LOUISE:

Thelma and Louise, now in their thirties, are home-town buddies from way back, Now, Thelma is married to a jerk, and Louise can't get away from her life as a waitress, single, and haunted by a rape in another city a long time ago.

They get on the road for a fun weekend to a cabin Louise has the key to. But, when they stop at a roadside cowboy dinner and dance place, Thelma gives in to the charm of a local guy, to dance, but she gets a little smashed, and Louise finds her in the parking lot as she's being brutally raped by the charming cowboy.

With a gun in her purse, that she forgot she had (Thelma asks her to hold it for her because she doesn't know how to use it). Louise shoots the bastard, and suddenly they are in trouble. Feeling that they would not be able to find justice for killing somebody in a drunken sexual escapade, they jump into the car and take off... terrified.

Due to Thelma's impetuous way of getting into trouble and Louise's anger and fear of blind justice in a man's world, they get into one scrape after another making the situation worse. They decide to go to Mexico to escape the law, and when Louise calls Jimmy to bring her life savings of $6,000 to her, Thelma goes and loses it all when she is charmed again by a wandering cowboy con-man who takes the money while she's in the shower. Then, angry at herself for screwing things up, Thelma decides to rob a variety store, and now they are really in trouble, bandits on the highway of life.

A good cop, a smart state detective, keeps closing in on them, and he keeps offering

them the chance to turn themselves in, since
he sees how a murder charge might not stick.
But, in the end Thelma and Louise are victims
of their own fears of justice in a 'man's'
world, and they must make a choice on their
own fate. Surrender to the law or make a run
for it? And, in the end, they make the right
decision... for them.

*******   ************   ******

ANOTHER ONE PAGE IDEA - 2ND TRY
THELMA AND LOUISE

Two home-town girls, 30's, Thelma and
Louise, decide to get out of town to escape
the rigor of Thelma's stupid middle class
marriage to a butthead named Darryl; and the
haunted past of Louise who has had trouble
putting together a life with any man. She's
still a waitress, with a head on her
shoulders. Thelma is pretty much of an
airhead.

They run out of town (Arkansas town) and a
great sense of freedom overcomes them as they
get further into the potentials expressed
stretching out in beautiful landscapes ahead
of them. It's just them and nature. No men
to interfere. Or, are there...?

Thelma wants to have some fun... and
dances with a cowboy charmer at a roadside
dive. He gets her a little drunk and takes
her out to the parking lot. He's just about
to get into her pants, when...

Bam! Louise has a gun to his neck and
tells him to back off. He backs off, but
lips off at her... and she shoots him, dead.
Aghast, and not knowing just what to do, they
take off in Louise's car.

One thing after another happens, mostly
Thelma's fault, which Louise has to figure a
way out of, and it only gets worse as they

run from the law, afraid to give in, even to a good cop, who's on their trail and offers them some hope.

During the story, their relationships with men, especially Thelma's idiot, macho husband, and Louise's sometime boy friend, Jimmy, played out, and how these relationships and their past histories and also, how the traditional man-woman battle of the sexes forms their decisions are revealed to be at the base of an ironic story and it's evolving plot.

Make it a traditional movie chase plot, but with two women, and have that create a comment of it's own... how women in a man's world, even a man's movie, are in a dilemma not of their own making.

Let all these factors come together at the end when Louise and Thelma are caught by the police, and discover that being taken to jail is not their only option. They still are human and they still have choice.

THE 3 TO 5 PAGE STORY OUTLINE

This is where the chaff is separated from the wheat, where you will be tested for Character, Story Logic, Beginning, Middle, and End. And for Catalyst, Catharsis, Epiphany, remedy and Resolution. And you will be tested for clarity , theme, and the feel of the flow.

The process of writing a three to five page Story Outline is tricky and more extensive than a neophyte to the process can imagine.

The process I suggest is based on a combination of INTUITION and WRITING SKILLS. These writing skills are primarily an ability to construct and blueprint. This is harder when you are chomping at the bit.

First, write your ONE PAGE IDEA. Write it in one session of no more than fifteen minutes. Don't agonize over it. Let your intuition lead the way. Start anywhere, but START! It can be narrative or anything else. Put it in the form of a free association poem if you like. The main thing is to get the idea on paper.

Then, think about it, and do it again. Write the idea again. Write it another way, using what you have learned about your own idea from the first time you did it.

Do it again, start thinking about form and function. Your main character, how that character has a problem, how events can be arranged to introduce the problem and how the character acts and reacts, and then how events and character come together to resolve the problem in the end.

Still, don't let the ONE PAGE IDEA get away from you. Don't over write. Find a way to economize to keep it one page, maybe two at the most.

Now, hopefully, you're ready to attack the THREE TO FIVE PAGE OUTLINE. Start taking notes on ideas, form, character, the catalyst, theme, main points, style, etc.

OK, DO IT!
WRITE THE THREE TO FIVE PAGE OUTLINE.

Do it in one session of thirty minutes to an hour. No more. Blue pencil it with new ideas. Think about it. Think about what is missing, what is too much. Does it work? What's wrong with it? Show it to somebody you respect and trust. What is their instinct about it? What don't they understand?

A day or two later, repeat the process. Start from scratch. Do not use the first outline for reference! It is the mark of a good writer when he is willing to scrap old writing in favor of new. He doesn't try to cut and paste and hold onto favorite passages. He can do it again, and he can do it better. So start from scratch again, and write without stopping for an hour or a little more. Don't get trapped into stopping for some problem. You can fix that problem in the next draft. Just keep going. If you have a new idea which tends to change something you've already written, keep the new idea and you can change the original idea upon which it is dependent later.

Think about the outline again. Take notes. Ask for a valuable outside opinion. Then, a day or two later, do it again.

Repeat this process until you are thoroughly satisfied with the outline. It works! Make sure that another reader agrees that it works. Make sure that someone other than yourself is just a happy as you are with it.

Remember, the flaws in your Story Outline will be magnified ten-fold in your novel or screenplay, and fifty times in the movie if it gets made. Don't get trapped into loving what you have done. **Hate it.** Wonder what's wrong and what could be better. Does C follow B following A? Do the strings all tie together? Have I gone off on a tangent? Is the story on concept? Does the main character reflect my feelings as an author? Does the main character embody ideas and theme and conflict within his own character? Does this translate in the story and the plot? Has the situation I set up in the First Act caused a thrust throughout the story and right on through to the end? Have I created anything that is gratuitous? If so, find a way to integrate all the elements into a network of inter-dependent relationships.

For the Final Draft, you can allow yourself the luxury of incorporating ideas, paragraphs, etc. from earlier drafts.

AN EXERCISE -
THE THREE TO FIVE PAGE STORY OUTLINE
THELMA AND LOUISE

You may perform this exercise in one of two ways or both.

If you know the story of THELMA AND LOUISE, use you own way of outlining the story that you already know by completing the outline started below. Don't forget the catalytic event creating the thrust.

If you do not know the story of THELMA AND LOUISE, use the characters, relationship, situation and a catalytic event of your own creation to create a workable story outline.

THREE TO FIVE PAGE STORY OUTLINE - THELMA AND LOUISE

This is the heart warming, yet disturbing story of two women, home-town buddies, with an urgent desire to break free of the social restraints they have been placed on them as women in a "Man's" world.

One, Thelma, is impetuous and filled with pent up sexual desire. She is blinded and naive to the realities of life, and it would seem she has a subconsciously made life choices to suit that persona. A few years ago, she married Darryl, a macho man in sales, only to protect herself from her own impetuous nature. (Why else would a woman

marry a guy like Darryl?)   The other, Louise,
is Thelma's opposite... more worldly, she
removed her blinders long ago.   An attempted
rape in Houston some time back has haunted
her... and probably handicapped her in her
relationships with men.   She has a boy
friend, Jimmy, a musician on the road a lot,
who would like to be with her more, but she
maintains just enough distance from Jimmy to
keep him... AND to keep him away.   He's
useful when needed.

Together, these two are tinder and
match... so when they set out for an innocent
weekend romp, we already feel the tension.

And, soon enough...

O.K., NOW YOU FINISH IT.

SCENES -

Scenes have a beginning, middle and end. The beginning is the hypothesis and premise (what if?), the middle is the confrontation or catharsis of the situation, and the resolution is the payoff. Try to use props as symbol, and action and reaction more than dialogue. Use dialogue as a necessary evil, carrying the subtextual meaning of the scene forward. Let the payoff be visual and tactile if possible.

SCENES - THE STEP OUTLINE
This is useful like sketch work for a larger painting.
Sketch out the entire movie in steps. First in SEQUENCES, then break down sequences into scenes.

SEQUENCE 1 - Thelma and Louise decide to go out of town. Thelma tricks Darryl, and takes a gun almost by accident (why?). They feel free as they go in Louise's convertible.

SEQUENCE 2 - They pull into cowboy night club at Thelma's insistence. Louise is reluctant (because of what happened in Texas). Harlan, a cowboy stud, seduces Thelma to dance with him, gets her a little drunk, and takes her out to the parking lot. Louise can't find Thelma, finds her in the parking lot getting brutally raped. Puts the gun to Harlan's head, and shoots him when he sasses her. They take off. (Yeow... their lives will never be the same)

SEQUENCE 3 - On the road, Thelma is beat up and confused. Louise is trying to think. Reveal that Louise feels that, in a man's world, no one will believe their story. They have to run. Thelma's simply thinks they should call the police, but listens to Louise's greater worldly experience.
... cont. through to THE END.

STEP OUTLINE - SCENES
Now break down a sequence by breaking it into scenes.

STEP OUTLINE - INDIVIDUAL SCENES
SEQ. 4, SCENE 4 –

Night, car pulls up to Oklahoma motel.

Louise tells Thelma to wait in car.

Louise goes in, goes up to clerk, asks if there's been a telegram for her, or for "Peaches". Clerk says no, her face falls, Jimmy has failed her.

In the B. G., someone has been reading the newspaper, covering his face. It's Jimmy!

MORE EXERCISES:

CONFLICTS OF THELMA AND LOUISE: Write an explanation for each of the following conflict; then--

Take each CONFLICT through the three stages of beginning, middle and end.   In some instances, beginning, middle and end, may mean Past, Present and Future. So that the Catalyst may have happened in the past, the Catharsis is what's going on now, and the Epiphany must happen two-thirds through the movie, and as a result, the Remedy and Resolution. Here goes:

THELMA V. HERSELF (COVERT CONFLICT)

THELMA V. DARRYL

THELMA V. LOUISE

LOUISE V. HERSELF AND HER PAST

LOUISE V. THE LAW

LOUISE V. THELMA

LOUISE V. JIMMY

THELMA V.   COWBOY #1

THELMA V.   COWBOY #2

(How does her interaction with the cowboys reveal the conflicts in her psyche?)

THELMA AND LOUISE V.   A MAN'S WORLD (THEME)

THELMA AND LOUISE V. MEN

THELMA & LOUISE V. THE CHEMISTRY OF THEIR FRIENDSHIP

YIN AND YANG

ACTION AND REACTION

MASCULINE FEMININE

JACK AND JILL EXERCISE

Jack and Jill went up the hill
to fetch a pail of water
Jack fell dawn
and broke his crown
and Jill came tumbling after.

Create your own story of Jack and Jill. We know the essentials of the plot, but we don't really know anything else. Keeping the rules of the road in the back of your mind, use your instinct and intuition to write the story. Have fun!

When you are finished see how many of the following questions, you can answer. Which of the questions are not answered in the story you wrote? Okay, now do a second draft of the story from scratch, utilizing the new information.

REMEMBER; USE YOUR INTUITION FIRST; THEN ANSWER:

Who is Jack?

Who is Jill?

What is their relationship?

What is the conflict between them?

What is the conflict with the rest of the world?

Who is the antagonist?

Why are they going up the hill?

Is it only to fetch the water?

What happens at the top of the hill.

Do they get the water? Whose story is it, Jack's or Jill's?

Can it be both?

What is the First Act? What event is the catalyst?

What is the Second Act? How does Catharsis take place?

At the end of the second Act, what does Jack suddenly realize about himself, and-or his relationship with Jill?

What does Jill do to facilitate Jack's story? Is the story heading towards an inevitable, inexorable ending?

Is the story resolved?

Is the plot resolved also?
Did the story and the plot resolve synchronistically?
Did you know the ending at the beginning?
What is the raison d'être for your story?
Do you feel that the audience should be satisfied, having experienced catharsis.?
Is your Plot graphic and cinematic? Does it have scope?
Does the plot carry the story well?
Is the plot the equal of the story?
What music do you imagine as the score?
What actors could play the parts?

WRITERS BLOCK

Forget it. Writers Block isn't worth the paper it's not written on.

Sorry. I know writers block is very real for some people but I've never suffered from it.

Okay, so you're not "ready" to write. That's real. But what is it you're NOT ready to write. Instead of dwelling on that, dwell on the positive...what you ARE ready to write.

You aren't ready to write the scene, but you are ready to take notes on it, you are ready to write a sketch of what the scene is to be about...and maybe you are ready to write the scene and you don't know it. There's only one way to find out.

Write the scene.

Then write it again.

Sit down.

Write.

Write again.

Edit.

Write again.

Keep going.

Don't be afraid. It's not written in stone.

Blank page?

Fill it.

Do it again.

Let your characters write for you. Through you. They need you. You are their ride through the scenes and the acts. Act I, Sc. I., Act Two, Act Three. End.

Write through the acts. Each scene has a beginning, middle and end. Each character has a beginning, middle and end.

You don't need to know anything. If your mind is a blank, it means you have a clear head...ready for your muse and your characters to ride right through...onto the page.

If your mind is filled up, cluttered with junk, it means you can unload...you must unload. Sit down, start writing, get rid of that load.

See. There are no excuses.

Do it. Do it now.

ACT THREE
SCENE FOUR:

NOVELS &
PLAYS

WRITING THE PLAY
WHAT'S THE DIFFERENCE?

The difference between movie writing and playwriting is not, as one might think, that plays are "live", and therefore more immediate in their emotional impact. Such is not the operative differential.

The Proscenium Arch is the difference. More so than novels or movies, the proscenium arch behind which the actors must act out the drama separates the audience from the play and the players from the audience, creates a distancing from the "live" audience just as impactful as the written word creates a distancing between each individual reader/audience.

That is why a play is "presented". It is mounted and presented as a living painting, and it is your task as author to understand your own play as a painter would his painting.

Your play is confined within a framework, the proscenium arch, and even when the arch is supposedly broken, as in Arena Theatre, it is not really broken because the audience is constantly asked to reconstruct the arch through its own imagination It's asked to reconstruct the set and setting because the props are minimal. While arena style is meant to present the audience with greater immediacy and more emotional impact, it actually performs the opposite function. It puts a strain on the audience's imagination, and it presumes that the audience is too stupid to feel the emotions of the story if it's presented behind the arch. It is of course a matter of dramatic weight, and the important thing to understand is that it is the author's choice of dramatic weight, not the director's. If the author has written his play for the arena, so be it, but if the author,- Shakespeare, Arthur Miller, Eugene O'Neill,- has written his play for the stage, the director had better have a firm grip on his re-interpretation to present it otherwise. David Mamet's plays are more for the arena, I would think, and Miller's more for the stage.

YOUR WORDS FROM ANOTHER'S LIPS

And because the actors are live upon the stage, their performances are an act of authorship to either enhance or sometimes to reduce your own authorship as playwright. The audience does not perceive the author/writer, it perceives the actor/author...and so you are further distanced from your audience in the act of catharsis.

ON PLAYWRITING

For you, as a playwright author, you must use the rules of dramatic structure to your advantage, understanding and adapting the rules to the medium of playwriting.

DIALOGUE- BE DAMNED

Dialogue is the key. Unlike movies, which require Action and Reaction, and novels which require the reader's imagination to translate words into pictures and character, in a constant rapport between reader and author through the literate exposure of inner conflict and plot device - dialogue will be your foremost tool. Dialogue remains a form of exposing the deceits and conceits of your characters, and it is at one and the same time the vehicle for your story to move and thrust and the dead weight repository for the replacement of a movie's action and the weight of literature in the novel as background and a setting and plot which, in literature, moves through time and place at the easy behest of the author. Unlike movies, unlike novels, you are stuck with dialogue, so use it well.

Understand that it is not what is in the lines, but what is between the lines, the secrets between the author and the audience...secrets which the speaker of the dialogue may be trying to hide, or he may be carrying exposition as a weight to the revelation and thrust of his inner conflict. Plot must be spoken, wherein the novel or the screenplay, it can be described through action and movement.

And so, then, the balance between Story and Plot is uneasy. Because Plot should be kept to a minimum, and Story must be maximized, it becomes incumbent upon the playwright to carry the story forward with minimal action and minimum evolution of physical character. There is, indeed, more drama to be expected from a play, and more indeed is expected of the characters to reveal, when speaking, their thoughts and their secrets and their wishes and desires in interacted dialogue with other characters. In GLENGARRY GLEN ROSS, David Mamet is able to create constant flow of dialogue which moves the story along. Each character is fully realized through his speeches and his habits, smoking cigarettes, or the look in his eyes. Yet, when translated to the screen, it translates as a filmed play, not a cinematic movie.

MANIFESTATION OF CHARACTER TELLS THE STORY

In a play, you will need to flesh out the drama of your character, replay the theme and variations of your theme almost entirely through character. Character will wield Story and Story will wield Plot, through dialogue, and, in the end, it will be the manifestation of Character more so than the story or plot which must carry the emotional content to the audience. They will love and hate the people, they will laugh and cry at the humanity and human foibles and human frailty and humanness of the characters. Story will follow Character on a string, and the cathartic interplay between the main character and the audience will be strong, but not "exciting" in the sense of a movie or novel, where the catalyst at the end of Act One is a physical event combining with an emotional conflict. In a play, the catalyst will be an unseen story element presented through dialogue and interacting with the emotional conflict of the main character, creating a different sort of catalytic reaction.

SCOPE AND DEPTH

Keep your breadth narrow and your depth deep.

The narrower the scope the better, and the deeper the depth of your theme, you character, your story, the better. Opera and Musical Comedy (e.g. LES MISERABLES) can handle some scope, historical backdrops for example, but not so well as movies can. So try to keep the scope within a narrow context of plot and theme. A day-in-the-life will play better than a lifetime. Saroyan set THE TIME OF YOUR LIFE in a bar, and O'Neill did the same with THE ICEMAN COMETH, in 'real' time, about three hours. Expanded time requires device, which takes up time and space and more plot, rather than less. In a play, Less is More. And the more you have less, the greater the depth of what you do have.

Depth is the key in any case. It opens the door to the audience, makes the catharsis plain and simple, and gives the proscenium arch a chance to maintain its frame around the painting in a manageable size. After that, Story and Catharsis become the issue. Emotional issues which give all the collaborators, author, player, director, scene designer, and of course, audience, a better chance to do its job.

ON FORM

If you want to learn the form of plays, read plays and emulate and adapt the forms which suit you. Better yet, try your hand at authorship....invent your own form. Transform the stodgy stage and excite the world of Theatre.

ON NOVEL WRITING
"HE" OR "ME"?

OOPS, IT'S "YOU" AGAIN.

The same dynamic principles of writing dramatically apply to novel writing as to screenwriting or playwriting, but with some very important exceptions.

AUTHORSHIP BECOMES EVEN MORE PRONOUNCED IN THE NOVEL.

Authorship is all the audience gets. There are no go-betweens the writing and the reading. What the reader reads is what he gets. He does not get a translation to the screen. He does not get an interpretation of the author's words through actors on a stage. And authorship is all the author gets too. He must live with his words. He can take all the credit, and he must suffer all the blame.

Every decision you make has a multiple impact on the reader, and it is your decision alone. No director, no studio, no actors, no popcorn. Just you and your Muse.

FIRST PERSON FIRST

The key decision you have to make at the very beginning is whether to tell the story in the First Person or in the Third Person. First Person is "I". ("Call me Ishmael"--the first line of MOBY DICK) Third Person is "He" of "She". ("Sam Spade holed up in his second floor office, nursing the bump on his head, the neon sign of the bar across the street blaring like a disgruntled trumpet in his waterlogged mind. Still, he had figured out who the man with the black fedora was... and so maybe it was worth a knock on the noggin.")

"I", of course, is more immediate. You, as author, are putting yourself right on the line. It is subjective, introspective. Both the plot and the story are through your eyes. "He" makes you, as author, the observer.

The plot is through "his" eyes, but the story is through yours.

"ACROSS THE ROOM WAS THE MAN WHO KILLED MY FATHER."

When Allan Folsom's first novel, THE DAY AFTER TOMORROW, sold to its publisher for $2,000,000, Folsom explained that he had discovered his story in the very first paragraph, using the "I', perhaps knowingly, perhaps it was serendipitous, he was getting right inside the protagonist and his inner conflict; setting as the scene in a European cafe, nursing a glass of wine, his protagonist suddenly spots--"**across the room was the man who killed my father.**"

Dynamite! In his first paragraph, he hits the Mother Lode: told in the universal terms of a son and a father, a son whose inner conflict related not only to the murder of his father but to the psychological forces of the Oedipal conflict raging in his own soul, whereby, to become a "man", a son must "kill" his own father, not in fact, but psychologically, and, in this case, the need to avenge his father's murder (if it was that) in a confrontation with his father's killer.

After that first paragraph, where he states his premise, his theme and his conflict all at once, the author's task became one of plotting, because the story surely would yield itself from the inner conflict of the main character; and indeed, so admits the author, the novel started to write itself.

Had Folsom chosen the "He" instead of the "I" to tell the story, it would have lost this impact. If Dasheil Hammett had told the Sam Spade stories in the "I" instead of the "He", perhaps the twists and turns of the plot, and most especially, the author's ability to pick and choose when and how to explain Sam Spade's inner conflict would have lost their spark. Erle Stanley Gardner created Perry Mason in the Third Person. But, on the other hand, Mickey Spillane used the "I" technique. In fact, his most famous detective thriller was called, "I, THE JURY."

THE POWER OF DRAMATIC WEIGHT

"I" is the most internal device an author can use, and in a novel it can be incredibly powerful. In fact, the choice you make has to do with Dramatic Weight, just how powerful you want the device to be. "Mother died today" is the first line of Albert Camus' existentialist classic, THE STRANGER. It is written in the "I", yet he created a protagonist who doesn't say "MY mother died today." Purposely, Camus creates a character who tells his story in the First Person, but he is a man who has surrendered his subjectivity. His feelings have become numb, existential by definition, and the character himself takes on the devise of the Second Person. It is a powerful reconstruction of the device, revealing how manipulative an author can be in making his choices.

The choice of "He" does offer less dramatic weight to internal conflict that the choice of "I", but the power of the medium of the novel itself to reveal inner conflict still gives the author great authority.

Author-ity.

POWER OF THE NOVEL FORM

The inherent power of the novel it its ability to bring the internal affairs of its main character to the audience, and, for the author, to choose when and how to strike at the audience with not only the internal affairs of the character, but their interpretation.

THE AUTHOR OF A NOVEL HAS MORE CHOICE

Essentially, the author of a novel, has more choice. He has more control. He has more Time, in fact, time doesn't matter. He can stroll or he can move urgently, as dictated by his characters. More than any other medium the author can depend on his characters to tell their story for him...he can act as a translator, writing down their thoughts, and then reforming them into his own mirrored image and putting them on his track and letting it go.

You have that power. The words will be there when you need them.

NOVEL IS LITERATURE

Ultimately, the novel is more literature than drama. Your connection with the audience is directly through your words, unencumbered by scenes and dialogue actually meant to be spoken out loud. So too are your own words which carry Dramatic Weight, and you can create breadth and depth and meaning with every word. Your audience is your reader, and he reads at his own pace, mulls the meanings, and you are in a direct relationship with that reader. Your protagonist is as much of a messenger as a potential hero, and the demons of his inner conflict can be explained in more ephemeral terms than the direct Action and Reaction mechanics necessary to a strong screenplay. You and your reader become one, and you share the story of the main character between you.

Whereas in a movie, you cannot get away with presenting it in a literary way, in a novel you cannot get away with superseding literature with drama. Earlier, I wrote of how the literary nature of OF MICE AND MEN could not translate well dramatically to the screen. And, conversely, let's say, Spike Lee's "auteur" movies, DO THE RIGHT THING, SHE'S GOTTA HAVE IT!, SCHOOL DAZE, and MO' BETTER BLUES are movies that play cinematically, and that's that. They could be staged, they could be written as novels, but they would not likely translate well dramatically, nor would they translate well into literature.

AUTHORSHIP IS A STATE OF MIND

Authorship is a state of mind. It can be applied to any art form- movies, stage, novels, painting, dance, rock music, opera...you name it. Each medium requires the same structural story telling approach, only in different tones. Perhaps only the authorship of poetry is more specific and refined than Novel writing. You control with words, and words are even more specific than brush strokes with colors. Given that power with words, your state of mind becomes your greatest asset, and the keys are Passion and Intuition.

So, want to write the Great American Novel? Go ahead. Do it. No one is stopping you. No one stopped Alan Folsom, or E.M. Forster, or John Steinbeck, or Stephen King, or Herman Melville.

UNRESTRICTED BLUEPRINTING

When you write a movie or a play, you are more like an architect, blueprinting your scheme within very specific parameters of time and space. You have no such parameters in novel writing. You can make the novel as long as you like, or as long as the story dictates, and in as many volumes as you wish. Your authorship is unfettered by any restrictions of form and style, time or place, whatsoever. Your art is in a pure form. James Joyce. Dostoevky. Salinger. Their art is pure, their greatness secured in the medium they chose, and one of the tests of their authorship is that their works do NOT translate well to movies or stage.

STILL, IT'S THE SAME

No matter what, the same basic rules of writing dramatically apply to writing novels. Inner Conflict yields Character which yields Story, which yields Plot. Three Acts. A Catalyst at the end of Act One, yielding Crisis and Catharsis, then Epiphany; and finally, Remedy, Climax and Resolution. The audience must be satisfied through its own catharsis. The Holy Trinity applies, that Story is emotional and Plot is physical applies. You can bend theses rules more in a novel than any other medium, but you can't break them.

CHOOSE YOUR POISON

If you choose to write in the novel form, you will have more freedom than any other form. Still, you will have to have the linguistic and artistic tools to write in a clear and literary way, yet be able to convey the emotional content and construction from beginning to end.

Take Jack Kerouac. Did he have literary tools when he was simply writing in coarse language, poor grammar, and in free associative construction. Yes. ON THE ROAD has a beginning, a middle and an end for Sal, its conflicted protagonist, and the literary tools he used created a style which complements the story. E.M. Forster, in his brilliant and very clear literary use of words, also created a style that suited his novel, but would have served Jack Kerouac poorly, and of course, vice versa. Yet, as authors, they share the same use of intuition, building of character and other aspects of the novel. In fact, E.M. Forster wrote a book entitled ASPECTS OF THE NOVEL. It is the best book I've ever seen on the subject. Read it.

ACT THREE
SCENE FIVE:

THE BUSINESS SIDE

"PARANOIA! I WAS AFRAID OF THAT!"

COPYRIGHT, PLAGIARISM AND THE CREATIVE RIGHTS OF AUTHORS

Paranoia is a two edged sword. It is on the one side self-defeating and on the other side it is self-protective. I recall a cartoon where a patient jumps up from the couch in his analyst's office, crying-"Paranoia! I was AFRAID of that!"

And so, your natural fear that your idea or your work might be stolen, is, unfortunately founded in truth. Ideas are stolen. But, it is also true that your idea may be simultaneously worked on by someone else without any knowledge of what you are doing, and vice versa. "Ideas," per se, "are a dime a dozen." What really counts is the execution of ideas, so be careful of basing your paranoia on ideas alone. Once your fears are past the "idea" stage, you need not worry too much about your realized WRITTEN work being plagiarized. You might worry more about your having infringed, unwittingly, on someone else's rights.

PROTECTING YOUR COPYRIGHT

The key legal factor is called "copyright." Your copyright is legally established the moment your work is tangibly expressed, even verbally. When you "publish" your work, even if only a few copies to show friends, you have established copyright, and you have nailed down that copyright by giving "notice of copyright" on the work, e.g. (c) 1993 Bill James Smith, Phoenix, AZ.

You can register your copyright by sending a copy of the work to The Copyright Office, U.S. Government, Washington D.C., and paying the appropriate fee. This gives you further protection.

Copyright can be transferred by sale or the licensing of various rights under the copyright. When AT&T makes a Mickey Mouse Telephone, it has licensed the right to do so from Disney. When Disney makes a movie from the fairy tale of BEAUTY AND THE BEAST, it may do so without the "author's" permission because this old fairy tale is in the PUBLIC DOMAIN. Anyone may use it. You may use the title and the basic story of Beauty and the Beast, but if you use the dialogue and original story structure of Disney's BEAUTY AND THE BEAST, you will have infringed on Disney's copyright.

If you are writing about real persons, living or dead, you must have the right to do so. Any living persons must grant you the right, or waive their rights. If you are writing about a dead person, you may have the right to write about that dead person, but if you are using subordinate characters that are still living you may need their permission to publish material with that person's character represented. If you write about Elvis Presley for example, who is dead, you may have that right, but if you "invent" a wife for him, his real wife or children, who are living, might have the right to sue you for Invasion of Privacy.

The best advice is--when in doubt, consult an attorney specializing in copyright law.

PLAGIARISM- YOU AND 'THEM'
You must worry a little about plagiarism, not just that someone may be stealing your idea, but that you may be infringing on someone else's copyright. Be careful that the dream you had last night about murdering your husband and running off with your boyfriend is not the very same story as THE POSTMAN ALWAYS RINGS TWICE. And when using characters who are similar to living persons, be careful that your thin veil of fiction cannot be pierced.

If you have an idea, it is best not to mention it to people other than trusted friends, and then, only if you are looking for their input. If a friend gives you input, he or she may have created an implied copyright on the content of their verbal contribution. The best thing to do is to put your idea in writing before you tell it to anyone else, and then add new elements to the written work as you think of them. Remember, the idea itself cannot be protected, and even worth more to remember, ideas are nearly worthless anyway. It is the written work that counts.

If you write or pitch "This is the story of a woman who emigrates to America in 1895, leaving her family behind, and works hard to bring her family, one by one to America" That's a non-copyrightable idea. But if you write,- "My Great Aunt Berthe looked at the Statue of Liberty with hope in her heart, and a tied-up babushka brimful with two salamis, a loaf of bread, a fading photo of the fifteen family members left behind in the gray ghetto of Pinsk, not to mention her mother's handwritten recipe for sweet pickles, slung over her strong right shoulder. Perhaps she knew even then how valuable that pickle recipe would become...because she had hope. She felt it in her heart, this was America." -- you have a copyright that is protectable.

COLLABORATION WITH ANOTHER WRITER

Collaboration is a dangerous area. If you collaborate with someone and then have a breakdown in your relationship, or disagree artistically, it may be difficult to establish which of you has the copyright on the material.

If you are going to collaborate from your idea, you should make an agreement in writing before you begin as to who has the copyrights in the event of a breakdown between you. If it is your idea and you are an accomplished writer, you will want to protect yourself by insisting that the idea revert to you in the event of a breakdown, and that when a completed work by you is sold or published or produced, that the person you were working with will receive no credit, but his or her contribution will be compensated for at a set price or as a percentage of your earnings from the copyright. If a breakdown in the collaboration occurs in the late stages of the collaboration, you may have little or no recourse but to honor a fully shared collaboration in both credit and in compensation. What you can do in a written agreement before you begin, (if it is from your idea and you have enough "clout") is hold the right to control the business future of the copyrighted work without consultation with your collaborator. If there is then a breakdown, one partner will be unable to block the other from pursuing the business future of the work.

Personally, I do not collaborate, and one of the reasons is that it presents too many legal problems. A better reason is that I prefer to work alone. Except where certain areas of expertise may come into play from your collaborator, I feel that collaboration is really a form of hand-holding to fend off the fears of writing by yourself. And, above all, once you choose to be an "author" rather than a writer, you will work alone.

Your best protection in submitting to producers, studios, and publishers is to contract with a recognized Literary Agent who may submit your work under his protection. Lists of Literary Agents are available from the Writers Guild of America West in Beverly Hills, Ca. for TV and movies producers; or the Writers Guild of America East in New York City for book publishers.

If you are a "writer for hire" in Hollywood, you are considered to be a participant in the creative and collaborative process. You have certain rights in this process, most of which have been gained over many years of painful strikes and negotiation by the Writers Guild of America. The least of these rights is copyright. Copyright is most valuable to novelists and playwrights and of minimal value to writers for hire. Practical rights, negotiated through the Writers Guild's Basic Agreement with studios and recognized producers who have signed the Basic Agreement, and then further negotiable by you and your agent, depending on your "clout" are more important to you than copyright. You may learn what they are in a pamphlet prepared by the Writers Guild, called CREATIVE RIGHTS FOR WRITERS OF FILM AND TELEVISION.

To register your copyright with the government, call the Copyright Hotline, 24 hours a day. 202- 707- 9100.

You may register your work with the Writers Guild of America even if you are not a member. This is not to copyright your work, but to establish a date of registration. Call the Writers Guild HotLine at 310-205-2500.

Above all, remember that you will be able to retain more rights and have greater bargaining power when you have developed your idea into a strong, well written work. Try not to put the cart before the horse, don't try to sell your work before it is written.

LITERARY AGENTS AND PUBLISHERS

Legitimate Publishers and Producers generally depend on legitimate Literary Agents for submissions. Publishers and Producers trust that a legitimate Literary Agent will only submit manuscripts and screenplays that he has read and can recommend.

Therefore, you are dependent upon finding a Literary Agent who will read your work, and, if he likes it, recommend it to a publisher or producer.

If you are not yet established, it will be a difficult process to find a legitimate Literary Agent who will even read your work. For novels and plays, you will want to find a Literary Agent in New York; and there are some in Chicago and Los Angeles, and one or two in most large American Cities. In New York, the Dramatists Guild may be able to provide you with a list of recommended agents. In Los Angeles, the Writers Guild of America has a list.

Beware of agents who ask for a fee to read your work. Most legitimate agents do not require a fee. The Scott Meredith Agency in New York is a large legitimate agency that will read your work for a fee, and many first novels have gone through the Meredith reading process and found their way to a publisher on Meredith's recommendation.

Take heart. If you have written a good novel, play or screenplay, somehow it will find its way. The many stories of rejection after rejection and then finally acceptance and publication are true. Talent will out, and the cream will rise to the top.

Hollywood is hungry for good scripts, and New York is hungry for great novels and the reason that so much money is paid for good scripts and novels is that it is, for Producers, like finding a needle in a haystack. If you write one worthy of production, it will rise to the top through the publisher's or producer's reading process. The reading process is stoked by legitimate literary agents submitting scripts to producers, studios, and publishers.

Do not attempt to sell ideas and story outlines in Hollywood unless you are an established writer signed with an established literary agent. If you have a script to be read, literary agents WILL read it. If you are a newcomer, you would be smart to ferret out a less established literary agent, one who is hungrier for good scripts that a high-profile agent. Even then, the larger agencies have Story Departments with readers waiting to read or, at least, glance over, every script that comes in.

Once an agent becomes interested in your work, he may want to sign you to a contract to represent you. By law, if he produces no results within 90 days, the contract becomes null and void. If he or she does not sign you to a contract, do not allow the agent to "shop" your work anywhere, unless it is a one-stop submission for a specific reason, well explained by the agent.

Finally, be ruthlessly objective about your own work. If a general consensus finds fault with it, listen. Most Literary Agents are experienced analysts. They know how your work stacks up in the market. They know the difference between a saleable, produceable work and one which needs work. You can trust their judgment. Listen.

ACT THREE: SCENE SIX

THE WRITERS FUTURE

THE LAST WORD

THE WRITER'S FUTURE

Better than ever, American writing techniques are sought and taught worldwide. Certainly in the realms of film and TV is it so. American entertainment is a major export to the rest of the world, and American writing technique is the sine qua non of American styled entertainment. While this book applies to a concept of 'Authorship' which often seems to run contrary to "writing for hire," the principles of Authorship can be applied in great measure to works written for hire. Sometimes that measure can be very great, witness all the film scripts that have been nominated for Academy Awards in the category of "Written for the screen, adapted from another medium."

While I would not give the writer of these works the title 'Author', I would suggest that the principles of authorship have generally been applied in a marriage between two authors, each of whom needed the other, and one of whom found inspiration in the other. Think of it as part of The Holy Trinity, where an 'ecstatic' rapport has been established between two writers.

It was once thought that European "films" were better than American Movies, and before Melville and Thoreau, it was thought that European fiction and authorship were superior as well. Those prejudices have gone out with clipper ships, in the one case, and Spam, in the other. Ingmar Bergman inspired Woody Allen, Eisenstein taught Coppola and Lucas and Spielberg...in such a way that the so-called European sensibilities have been blended into American 'action' movies. There are those who still believe that "character" is better off in the hands of the Europeans. I disagree. The Americans carry character into the realm of action in a time tested way that seems to elude the rest of the world, (except for Kurosawa in Japan.) The twain has met...and it is on the shores of America.

In the area of novels, there is a history of American authorship, from Herman Melville to Stephen King which is just as symbolic and just as meaningful as the authorship of novels elsewhere around the world. Still the American techniques of Detective Stories, potboiling romance novels, and other 'genre' seems to be uniquely exportable. And the envy of the rest of the world.

TECHNOLOGY FORETELLS THE FUTURE

Interestingly, George Lucas, whose STAR WARS movies and whose techniques of Special Effects have revolutionized movies, predicts that even newer technology will soon change the way writers think. He speaks of how Special Effects will soon no longer be restricted to what must be built (e.g. big sets and monstors) in order to be cinematographed for the screen. Instead the image can be produced as a computer generated graphic, animated like "real", then transposed to video or film. Imagine not having to build King Kong, but simply creating King Kong and his jungle on a computer screen, with 'movement' correspondent to real life movement. Unlike animation, you will not be able to distinguish from reality. Next, there will be no need for actors and actresses and extras....ooops, that's going too far.

Think about Charles Dickens, his 19th Century novels were serialized in a weekly newspaper, and it was that technique for publication which caused him to write A TALE OF TWO CITIES in a serialized format. Hmm..perhaps the serialized novel will return in response to the computer technology of the future, when electronic newspapers appearing on a flat, portable 9 x 12 inch screen at home are predicted to replace the news on paper. Perhaps a new demand for serialized stories will emerge. Perhaps the fans of DAYS OF OUR LIVES who don't have time to watch TV in the daytime will want to read a daily edition by keystroking DL/TV on their computer keyboard.

BIG BROTHER IS A FRUSTRATED WRITER

Playwrights, take heart. What about the three-dimensional holograph? Remember in STAR WARS, when the Wookie and Luke Skywalker were playing a chess-like boardgame with laser-holographically produced 3-D images of the characters-- 'live' pieces of the game moving from one square to another on the game board. Well, should such technology come true, you will be able to write plays that can be ordered up in one's living room, where the audience sits around arena style to watch the characters strutting around in their pettiest pace. Or even grandest pace...your imagination will be the limit of what characters might appear and what they can do.

Imagine that!

If this sounds like Big Brother to little-old-you, think about the benefits on the Little Brother side. You can't get a big monolithic publisher to publish your work, but you might be able to find a small one, even if it's...yourself. The electronic revolution includes techniques of desktop publishing and typesetting and printing allowing you to simply and inexpensively publish in small runs. The marketing side encourages small 'niches', where your work can successfully make a profit.

In the movies, similar revolutions have and will continue to make the little squirrel able to survive in the big forest. A computer generated movie, without actors, need not be expensive...you will be able to make it using your own equipment, from screenplay to release print....as a video. Perhaps it won't make it to the big videostores, but your marketing 'niche' will appear for you--selling it to a small distributor, who in turn could advertise it in small specialty publications, even on computer modem Billboards already extant.

So, author, be not dismayed that the electronic world will replace you like robots on the assembly lines. To the contrary, you with dreary jobs on the assembly lines will be freed by the robots to become humanized artistes, successfully plying your authorship in any way you choose.

There are no excuses. The markets are there. Decentralization, electronics....fax, modem, the home office...makes communication easy and inexpensive for a one man or one woman operation.

You're in the driver's seat.

Carpe diem.

THE VERY LAST WORD

Authorship is your divine right and privilege, like the divine right of Kings. You are self-endowed with creative ability. The dynamic principles of writing dramatically and creatively are discoveries I've made through my own personal experience. I have been your pathfinder and your trail blazing guide. If you get on the path, you will find your way to your creative center. You will discover that you can write.

Like music, which has a format consisting of bars, notes and staffs, time and interpretative instructions---- "pianissimo", "with feeling", and the like---writing has its formats and methodology of craft.

Use the formats, use craft, but use it intuitively. When a child is learning to read and play music, he must first learn to play mechanically, keeping in mind, in fact reading the music note by difficult note; but when he becomes a full-fledged musician, he plays effortlessly, with little or any reference to the academic elements of notes and bars and 4/4 time. He is more concerned with interpretation. When he finally translates this into being a creative force unto himself, using his creative will and his intuition and his inner feelings to produce the impetus by which he translates the the work in his heart and mind into singular, technical notes and bars in 4/4 time.

THE FINAL INGREDIENT-EXPERIENCE

The final ingredient to create your credential as an Author will be EXPERIENCE. You need never give up. Your first work is likely to be just that...a first work. But your third and your seventh and your last work may be masterpieces. When you combine your knowledge of the rules with your intuition and add the final ingredient of experience, your authorship will be ensured.

For any artiste, it is the complete body of his works which makes his total statement. Hemingway created a body of works that will stand for all time, and when he blew his head off, he added to the statement, no doubt intentionally. What an author! Great art has risks for the artist because he is putting himself on the line. Still, you can put your "self" on the line, make a statement through your work, and live to luxuriate in the glow of your accomplishments. Hemingway to the contrary. Be encouraged just to know that if your first work doesn't succeed or is less than what you intended, the second work will be better and the third even better. Suddenly, wow! You've created a "body of works", and you are an author.

Stay centered. Stay your course. Don't second guess the market. Don't second guess what a movie studio is looking for. They really don't know. Don't let the market dictate what you will create. If you do, you will become theirs. The status of Authorship must be guarded. It's yours. No one can take it away. Only you can allow it to be taken.

Finally, do not depend on me, do not depend on what I have written. Use it as a guide, not a crutch. Read it, learn from it, then use it as it suits you. The Cannon Planagram, for example, is not gospel; it's just a format. Use it extensively, partially, or not at all. It's up to you.

Keep in mind the bare essentials. Beginning, Middle, End. Thrust, Battle, Payoff. Feel "catharsis" and share it with your audience. Understand that there are ways to avoid pitfalls and basic flaws--by outlining and double checking the classical dramatic structures   and techniques. But, don't be a slave. Be free, and be smart. Use craft for what it's worth ....to you.   If you must blaze a new trail, I support you.

Try to maintain the FEELING of authorship, the "ecstatic rapport" you want to create between yourself and your audience. Feel the alternating currents of Yin and Yang.   See how it feels, right now! How it feels, right now, to join me, as author of this book, in an ecstatic rapport as we move together to experience those two little words that represent our completion of the task. Ready?

THE END

EPILOGUE
THE CANNON
PLANAGRAM:
AN ORGANIZATIONAL
SYSTEM
for writers of screenplays,
novels, and plays

THE CANNON PLANAGRAM:
AN ORGANIZATIONAL SYSTEM
for the writer of screenplays, novels ,and plays

The Planagram is designed to be used with Index Cards. Give each index card a code corresponding to the "Y" vertical and the "X" horizontal. For Example "D-11" would be your comments about a "PLOT" element occurring in the beginning of the Second Act in that time frame known as "CRISIS" and "RE-NEW".

To further the system, you could COLOR CODE your index cards according to TIME FRAMES. ACT ONE, EXPOSITION, for example could be all Blue Cards running down the entire vertical through fifty or sixty numbered STORY AND PLOT ELEMENTS.

If you have a computer, and you know how to program it for keystrokes, you could create The Planagram as an Index Program on the Spreadsheet program of your computer. Then, you could create key-stroke "index cards" in a DataBase. Key stroke "D-11" on the Spreadsheet PLANAGRAM and the Data Base Index Card corresponding to D-11 will come up on the screen, and you can add to it as you desire.

You could also key-stroke all the Color Coded index cards corresponding to the "D" down column to appear on your screen all at once. So, when you are working on the First scenes of Act TWO, all your notes will appear at once.

The Planagram is a way to organize your notes and your thoughts. You must be the judge as to how much you want to depend on it. Don't let it become a crutch, slowing you down. Use it at the level you feel comfortable with, minimally. Don't use it at the expense of trusting in your intuition.

If you want to use the Planagram grid as a giant reminder on your bulletin board, you have permission to enlarge the Planagram by photocopying and enlargement. Enlarge it by as much as 500%.

Unlike Computer Screenwriting Programs costing hundreds of dollars, The Cannon Planagram is both a cost-free and a CREATIVE system. Design it according to your own needs.

PLANAGRAM INDEX CARD CODE

(Use this form on index cards, or program into keystroke index program on your computer.)

ELEMENT _____ CODE _____

ACT/SC _____ CODE _____

Color Code _____

RELATIONSHIP # 1: Thelma and Louise
Old friends before Thelma's marriage. BACK STORY:
Worked together at the Diner. Partied together. Grew up in the same home town.

Their relationship changed when Thelma got married, more distant. They want to re-vitalize their friendship without men in the equation. Louise's secret--i.e. what happened in Houston?--created some distance. Thelma's coupon cutting wifehood is irritating to Louise. The long term and the depth of their friendship is so strong that it will probably survive obstacles to come. In fact, the strength of such bosom buddies is that each would die or kill for the other if it ever came to that.

NOTE: As the story unfolds, show and do MANY OBSTACLES and despite that, the roots of their friendship hold, FORESHADOWING (SEE FORESHADOW _____) that in the end, the do KILL and they do KILL for each other. THIS IS AUTHOR'S SECRET, LET THE AUDIENCE FEEL THIS, BUT NOT KNOW IT UNTIL, AT THE END, IT IS SOLID BACKGROUND TO ALLOW AUDIENCE TO ACCEPT THE FINAL SOLUTION TO THEIR DILEMMA.

CROSS REFERENCE:
CHARACTER #1
CHARACTER #2
FOLLOW 'RELATIONSHIP #1-(_____) THROUGH ALL ACTS AND SCENES.
FOLLOW 'PLOT #1'-(_____) THROUGH ALL ACTS AND SCENES."
COLOR CODES
FORESHADOW/PAYOFF

SAMPLE OF HOW TO SET UP FILE CARD

THE CANNON PLANAGRAM.

A Checklist of Elements in Blueprinting a Story or Screenplay

Use the Planagram as a reference guide to your Index Card System
Use a different color-coded card for each Act/Sequence (A, B, C, Etc.) then cross-reference the Vertical List of "Story Elements"

The Index Cards are the Main Index Reference Guide.

ELEMENTS	A	B	C	D	E	F	G	H	I	EPILOGUE
	PROLOGUE	ACT ONE		ACT TWO			ACT THREE			
		SC/SEQ1	SC/SEQ2	SC/SEQ4	SC/SEQ5		SC/SEQ6 & SC/SEQ7			
		Set-up	Catalyst	Crisis	Catharsis	Ephiphany	Denoument - Climax - Resolution			
	Pages	Pages	Pages	Pages	Pages	Pages	Pages	Pages	Pages	Pages
1) Idea										
2) Idea										
3) Raisin-d'etre										
4) Premise (What if?)										
5) Theme										
6) Authorship										
7) Message										
8) Story										
9) Story										
10) Back Story										
11) Plot										
12) Plot										
13) Build Tension										
14) Pace (pages +)										
15) SubPlot1										
16) SubPlot2										
17) Maguffin										
18) Foreshadow										
19) Plant/Payoff										

CONFLICTS - conflict exists in very relationship, in every character, in every scene, via catalyst, catharsis and resolution.

THE CANNON PLANAGRAM - CONTINUED

	A	B	C	D	E	F	G	H	I	
	PROLOGUE	ACT ONE		ACT TWO			ACT THREE			EPILOGUE
		SC/SEQ1	SC/SEQ2	SC/SEQ4	SC/SEQ5		SC/SEQ6 & SC/SEQ7			
		Set-up	Catalyst	Crisis	Catharsis	Ephiphany	Denoument - Climax - Resolution			
ELEMENTS	Pages	Pages	Pages	Pages	Pages	Pages	Pages	Pages		Pages
20) Plant/Payoff										
21) Char 1 (Protagnst)										
22) Char 2 (Prot-aide)										
23) Char 3 (Antagnst)										
24) Char 4										
25) Char 5										
26) Char 6										
27) Relshp 1										
28) Relshp 2										
29) Relshp 3										
30) Relshp 4										
31) Action										
32) Action										
33) Turning Pt										
34) Turning Pt										
35) Turning Pt										

THE CANNON PLANAGRAM - CONTINUED

	A	B	C	D	E	F	G	H	I
	PROLOGUE	ACT ONE		ACT TWO			ACT THREE		EPILOGUE
		SC/SEQ1	SC/SEQ2	SC/SEQ4	SC/SEQ5	Ephiphany	SC/SEQ6 & SC/SEQ7		
		Set-up	Catalyst	Crisis	Catharsis		Denoument - Climax - Resolution		
ELEMENTS	Pages	Pages	Pages	Pages	Pages	Pages	Pages	Pages	Pages
REMINDERS									
36) Thrust									
37) Genre									
38) Dialogue									
39) Dialouge									
40) Metaphor									
41) Secrets									
42) Subtext									
43) Subtext									
44) Beats									
45) Time/Place									
46) P.O.V.									
47) Conflict									
48) Title									
49) Rythmn									
50) Magic									
51) Hear									
52) Soul									
53) Body									
54) Ambience									
55) Sope									
56) Inevitable									
57) Screen Time									
58) Myth-lines									

THE CANNON PLANAGRAM - CONTINUED

	A	B	C	D	E	F	G	H	I	
	PROLOGUE	ACT ONE		ACT TWO			ACT THREE			EPILOGUE
		SC/SEQ1	SC/SEQ2	SC/SEQ4	SC/SEQ5		SC/SEQ6 & SC/SEQ7			
		Set-up	Catalyst	Crisis	Catharsis	Ephiphany Denoument - Climax - Resolution				
ELEMENTS	Pages ___	Pages ___	Pages ___	Pages ___	Pages ___	Pages ___	Pages ___	Pages ___	Pages ___	Pages ___
59) Active										
60) Passive										
61) Detail										
62) Music										
63) Sound										
64) Camera										
65) Misc										
66) Misc										
67) Misc										

THE CANNON PLAN/DIAGRAM-SCENE BREAKDOWNS

ELEMENTS REMINDERS	A PROLOGUE Pages	ACT ONE		ACT TWO				ACT THREE	I Pages	EPILOGUE Pages
		B Set-up SC/SEQ1 Pages	C Catalyst SC/SEQ2 Pages	D Crisis SC/SEQ2 SC/SEQ4 Pages	E Catharsis SC/SEQ3 Pages	F Epiphany Pages	G Denouement Pages	H Climax - Resolution SC/SEQ6 & SC/SEQ7 Pages		
1) Thrust										
a. beat										
b. beat										
c. payoff										
d. page										
2) Thrust										
a. beat										
b. beat										
c. payoff										
d. page										
3) Thrust										
a. beat										
b. beat										
c. payoff										
d. page										
4) Thrust										
a. beat										
b. beat										
c. payoff										
d. page										
5) Thrust										
a. beat										
b. beat										
c. payoff										
d. page										
6) Thrust										
a. beat										
b. beat										
c. payoff										
d. page										

ADDENDA

READING LIST

PLAYS
Read the plays of Eugene O'neill, Arthur Miller, Eugene Ionesco, Edward Albee, David Mamet and others.

NOVELS
Read the novels of Herman Melville, Herman Hesse, Dashiell Hammett, Mary McCarthy, F. Scott Fitzgerald, Sterling Hayden. Stephen King, and whomever you favor.

SONGS
Read the lyrics of Frank Loesser, The Beatles, Bob Dylan, Carole King, The Grateful Dead, Johnny Mercer, Hoagy Carmichael and others.

SCREENPLAYS
THE   SCREENPLAYS OF JAMES AGEE (see film libraries),
"THELMA AND LOUISE" Callie Khouri, (not published, write M.G.M., Culver City , CA.
"BUTCH CASSIDY AND THE SUNDANCE KID"
William Goldman
Other Specific screenplays - Library of the Academy of Motion Pictures Arts and Sciences, Beverly Hills, Ca.

NON FICTION BOOKS

DRAWING WITH THE RIGHT SIDE OF THE BRAIN, Betty Edwards, 1979, Tarcher

ASPECTS OF THE NOVEL, E.M. Forster, 1956, Harcourt, Brace

POETICS, Aristotle, 1992, Prometheus Books

FILM AS ART, Rudolph Arnheim, 1957, University of California Press

INNER TENNIS, W. Timothy Galway, 1976, Random House

THE USES OF ENCHANTMENT: The Meaning and Importance of Fairy Tales,; Bruno Beitleheim, Ph.d. 1976, Knopf

THE POWER OF MYTH, Joseph Campbell, 1991, Doubleday

THE DRAMA OF THE GIFTED CHILD, THE SEARCH FOR THE TRUE SELF, Alice Miller, 1983, Basic Books.

AN ACTOR PREPARES, Constantin Stanislavski, 1948, Theatre Arts

FILM FORM, Sergei M. Eisenstein, 1969, Harcourt Brace

INDEX